Multiage
Classrooms
by Design

The Practicing Administrator's Leadership Series
Jerry J. Herman and Janice L. Herman, Editors

ROADMAPS
TO SUCCESS

Other Titles in This Series Include:

(see back cover for additional titles)

Multiage Classrooms by Design

Beyond the One-Room School

Tabitha Carwile Daniel
Kay W. Terry

CORWIN PRESS, INC.
A Sage Publications Company
Thousand Oaks, California

For information address:

Corwin Press, Inc.
A Sage Publications Company
2455 Teller Road
Thousand Oaks, California 91320

SAGE Publications Ltd.
6 Bonhill Street
London EC2A 4PU
United Kingdom

SAGE Publications India Pvt. Ltd.
M-32 Market
Greater Kailash I
New Delhi 110 048 India

Printed in the United States of America

Library of Congress Cataloging-in-Publication Data

Daniel, Tabitha Carwile.
    Multiage classrooms by design : beyond the one-room school /
Tabitha Carwile Daniel, Kay W. Terry.
        p.   cm. — (Roadmaps to success)
    Includes bibliographical references.
    ISBN 0-8039-6261-4 (pbk.)
    1. Nongraded schools—United States. 2. Classroom management—
United States.   I. Terry, Kay W.   II. Title.   III. Series.
LB1029.N6D36   1995
371.2'54—dc20   95-8842

This book is printed on acid-free paper.

95 96 97 98 99 10 9 8 7 6 5 4 3 2 1

Corwin Press Production Editor: S. Marlene Head

Contents

Foreword

Authors Tabitha Daniel and Kay Terry have produced a short, easily read book packed with excellent basic information about multiage classrooms. They share their personal expertise, research findings, the results of interviews with practitioners in multiage classrooms, and the valuable information they acquired as Kentucky implemented this concept, one that is growing in popularity across the United States for its research-based instructional delivery methods.

The book begins by stressing developmentally appropriate practice (DAP) that emphasizes the provision of a curriculum and an instructional delivery methodology that addresses the physical, social, intellectual, emotional, and aesthetic needs of young students and that also permits students to move through an integrated curriculum at the student's individual pace.

Chapter 1 delves into the history of multiage grouping as practiced during the one-room schoolhouse days, and the authors compare the one-room schoolhouse with the multiage classrooms of today. Chapter 2 explores the multiple roles and responsibilities of teachers in multiage classrooms. This outstanding chapter provides content related to (a) curriculum planning, (b) instructional delivery systems, (c) classroom organization, (d) classroom management, (e) student self-directed learning, and (f) peer tutoring.

Chapter 3 outlines the physical arrangements required to provide an effective environment for learning in a multiage classroom, and Chapter 4 sketches the roles and responsibilities of the principal assigned to a building that uses multiage classrooms.

The final chapter presents a compendium of comments from teachers, principals, parents, and community members about their perceptions of the multiage classroom in response to four interview questions administered by the authors. In addition, numerous references and a comprehensive bibliography of primary sources are included for those who wish to explore the subject of multiage classrooms in more depth.

Whether you are considering initiating a multiage classroom, are currently teaching in one, or are a principal of a multiage school, you will find this an enlightening, interesting, and very helpful book.

JERRY J. HERMAN
JANICE L. HERMAN
Series Co-Editors

About the Authors

Tabitha Carwile Daniel has 14 years of teaching experience in public schools in two states (preschool at-risk programs, kindergarten, and gifted education Grades 2 through 8). Her terminal degree is from George Peabody College of Vanderbilt University in Nashville, Tennessee. Currently, she is Associate Professor in Early Childhood/Primary Education at Western Kentucky University in Bowling Green, Kentucky.

She serves on the Kentucky Department of Education Primary Advisory Committee and chairs the Primary Education Task Force at Western Kentucky University. She is a consultant to numerous school districts and has presented at the local, state, and national levels on all aspects of multiage primary education and on the 1990 Kentucky Education Reform Act (KERA).

Working with teachers to plan and write integrated thematic studies and designing authentic assessment tasks for young children are two activities that she particularly enjoys.

She is an Institute Trainer for the Southern Early Childhood Association (SECA) programs: "An Appropriate Environment for Three- and Four-Year-Old Children" and "Developing an Appropriate Learning Environment for Children Five Through Eight Years Old."

She resides in Bowling Green, Kentucky, with her husband, Charles, and children, Wesley, Courtney, and Jordan.

Kay W. Terry is Assistant Professor at Western Kentucky University, where she has taught for the past 4 years. Prior to moving to Kentucky, she taught at the university level in Oklahoma. Her areas of expertise include early childhood, social studies, and language arts education. Terry has taught kindergarten and worked with students in gifted education in Grades K-12. Currently, she teaches undergraduate and graduate classes at both the elementary and secondary levels.

She has presented at the local, state, regional, national, and international levels in areas such as thematic instruction, whole language, authentic assessment, changes taking place as a result of KERA, and restructuring of teacher education programs. Terry is a member of cohort I of the KERA Assessment Fellows. Children's and adolescent literature is featured in many of her presentations. Her research interests include substitute teachers, the role of the principal, and whole language topics.

She is married to Richard Terry, and they have six children, ages 12 to 25. Her terminal degree is from Northwestern State University of Louisiana. She was born at Fort Knox, Kentucky, and grew up as an army brat, moving frequently. She loves to travel and find out about other people and other cultures.

Introduction: Multiage Grouping for Young Learners

Multiage grouping is placing children who are at least 1 year apart in age in the same classroom groups. The intent of multiage grouping in the 1990s is more than a convenience to accommodate increased or decreased enrollments of students to meet a desired class size ratio. Multiage grouping, when thoughtfully planned, can allow children of various ability and age levels to work and learn in an environment that is intended to optimize (a term coined by Lilian Katz) their learning potential.

The National Association for the Education of Young Children (NAEYC) in 1987 published *Developmentally Appropriate Practice in Early Childhood Programs Serving Children From Birth Through Age 8*. The document describes developmentally appropriate practice in early childhood programs for administrators, teachers, parents, policymakers, and others who make decisions about the care and education of young children. There are two aspects of developmental appropriateness: age appropriateness and individual appropriateness. Age appropriateness refers to the universally predictable sequences of growth and change that occur in children during the first 9 years of life. These changes occur in all domains of development—physical, emotional, social, and intellectual.

Individual appropriateness refers to the fact that each child is unique with a very individual pattern and timing of growth as well as an individual personality, learning style, and family background. Learning will occur as a result of interaction between the child's thoughts and experiences with materials, ideas, and people. To practice developmentally appropriate educational practices, a teacher must have a thorough understanding of child development and of the importance of age appropriateness and individual appropriateness to the designing of learning environments for young children.

Developmentally appropriate practice (DAP) means providing curriculum and instruction that address the physical, social, intellectual, emotional, and aesthetic needs of young learners and permits them to progress through an integrated curriculum at their own rate and pace. The knowledgeable teacher in a developmentally appropriate program will honor the development of the whole child. These teachers understand that children learn through active involvement and play. Teachers who practice DAP understand the social nature of learning and the role of language in mediating thought, communication, and learning.

Children are meaning makers, and they are constantly trying to make sense of their world. They do this by building new knowledge into their prior knowledge. They strive to connect or build their new knowledge with what they already know. Because each child is a unique individual with his or her own individual background, each child takes different information and makes different connections with the information learned. Each child will regulate not only what is learned but also the rate at which he or she learns.

Part 7 of *Developmentally Appropriate Practice* (NAEYC, 1987) describes DAP in the primary grades serving children ages 5 through 8. It is within the guidelines of developmentally appropriate evaluation for primary students that a case for multiaging is made.

> Children are not "promoted" nor do they "fail." Because children progress through sequential curriculum at different paces, they are allowed to progress in all areas as they acquire competence. Retention is avoided because of its serious im-

pact on children's self-esteem and the fact that the practice of retaining children in a grade for another year disproportionately affects male, minority, very young, and low-income children. The program is designed to fit the needs of the children: the children are not expected to change to fit the program. (p. 76)

In an article titled "Synthesis of Research on School Readiness and Kindergarten Retention," Lorrie A. Shepard and Mary Lee Smith (1986) highlight the research on retention, stating that "children who are the youngest in their first grade class have slightly lower achievement rates, but the difference is only 7 to 8 percentile points, and disappears by about third grade" (p. 80). The Southern Regional Education Board's (1994) *Getting Schools Ready for Children: The Other Side of the Readiness Goal* makes the following statements concerning retention:

Requiring students to repeat a grade because of poor performance is another familiar and widely accepted school practice in the United States. It is a practice that has little or no justification in terms of what we know about its effects. One review of the research on retention concluded that it [would be difficult to find another educational practice on which the evidence is so unequivocally negative]. (p. 22)

In *Getting Schools Ready for Children*, the following statement reinforces the concept that retention is inappropriate for young children:

Studies of children whose families choose to have them promoted even though teachers recommend retention or placement in transitional classes have found that the promoted children consistently perform as well as or better than their retained peers. Children who have been retained typically report less school enjoyment, demonstrate lower third grade achievement scores, and are more likely to drop out of school than those who have not been retained. (Southern Regional Education Board, 1992, p. 22)

Multiaging respects the wide range of developmental differences in young children. It allows children functioning below age group norms in some areas of their development to work with younger peers in a less stressful situation. The same is true at the opposite end of the spectrum for children who are functioning at above-age-norm levels. Teachers in multiage settings usually are more accepting of developmental discrepancies within children than are teachers in single-grade settings. Uneven development in children is considered normal, and teachers plan for teaching and learning situations that can enhance the child's motivation and self-confidence in the classroom.

Although the concept of multiaging and DAP is clear, implementing the practice requires administrators, teachers, children, and parents to rethink "school" as we have known it in the past. Multiaging has similar organizational components to heterogeneous, vertical, family, and ungraded or nongraded grouping, but the intent is different. In the past, the intent was to homogenize students by ability or developmental level grouping rather than by age grouping. Multiage grouping is now intended to maximize what can be learned when children of different, as well as same, ages and abilities have the opportunity to play, work, and learn together.

The One-Room School Revisited

At some time in our lives, probably during childhood, most of us remember listening to a relative telling stories about the conditions under which he or she went to school. If it was a grandmother or grandfather talking, a one-room school may have been the setting for the story. When we as adults talk about those memories today, we laugh about how the teller of those stories always walked at least 10 miles to school, uphill both ways, in the mud, rain, sleet, and snow, and so on. Although the exact details of those experiences may be cloudy, the ideas behind the one-room school were very specific. An education was an education. People then were glad to be able to go to school at all, and the conditions were far less important than the hoped-for outcome—an educated citizenry.

Today our modern schools are far removed from the one-room school of days past. Or are they? Why did we have these schools? Why did most of them disappear? Why might we today be looking back to this educational organization for ideas? Let's take a look.

The One-Room Schoolhouse

What Was It Like?

One-room schools represent the beginning of education in our country in the 1600s. Teachers were scarce, sending a child to school cost money, and students attended irregularly for a variety of reasons, including severe weather, distance to travel, perceived importance of schooling, and required work at home. School was frequently held in a building, such as a church, that already existed. Students sat on crude benches (later at desks) and worked from hornbooks (later slates and tablets). They memorized their lessons and recited them in turn during class. A large cast-iron stove heated the building in the winter. One of the older boys brought in the wood and fed the fire during the day. When it was hot, the window could be opened, but it was uncomfortable at times.

After textbooks were available, students used them (frequently shared) to study. Rote memorization and drill made up the curriculum. Students were grouped according to their capabilities, regardless of age. Attendance for some students was irregular. As a student achieved, he or she moved to another level or group. Teaching involved helping students learn the required curriculum, regardless of how long it took at any one level. Students of all ages worked in one room, some reading, some writing, some memorizing, and some reciting, all at the same time. They learned to work in this setting, concentrating on their own studies. If the teacher was busy, more capable students might help other students.

We had one-room schools for convenience and because of economic constraints. Not until there were more people in a given area, until the idea of publicly supported education was adopted, and until compulsory education came about was there a need or desire for multiroom schools in many locations. Approximately 70% of the schools in the United States in 1918 were one-room schools. Less than 1% of the schools in 1980 were one-room schools (Muse & Moore, 1988).

Why Did We Change?

Schools grew as the population grew, and students were broken up into smaller groups and, ultimately, into one-level grades for instruction. Teachers became better trained and specialized in levels of instruction and/or content areas of instruction. More attention was paid to what needed to be taught at each grade. Subject matter was the central focus as detailed curricula were developed for each grade in each content area. Schools became very business-like and took on more and more roles as society relinquished more and more of the responsibility it had held in the past to help develop good, moral, educated citizens.

There appear to be a variety of reasons why the change took place from the multiage classroom to the single-age or graded classroom. Anderson (1993) suggests that it came as a means of administrative practicality, having first been introduced by Horace Mann in Massachusetts. Mann initiated the idea in the mid-1800s, following the practices found in Prussia. It is suggested that one reason that gradedness became popular was the development of graded material such as the McGuffey reading series, five separate readers following one another in levels of difficulty (Ornstein & Hunkins, 1993). Blount (1992) writes that at first the implementation of separate grade classrooms separated children, but did not create the idea of set periods of time in a class followed by promotion or retention. However long it took to move to the next class, students advanced only when they were ready. Later, we developed the idea that all (or almost all) students could successfully complete the requirements for a grade of study in a set period of time. A growing population, compulsory attendance laws, and the overwhelming burden of financing schools all played major roles in creating the graded school we know today.

The Multiage Classroom Today

Yet today we see many schools and school districts—even entire states—returning to multiage, multigrade classrooms. The intent of multiage grouping in the 1990s is more than a convenience to accommodate increased or decreased enrollments of students to meet a desired class size ratio. Multiage grouping, when thoughtfully planned, can allow children of various ability and age levels to work and learn in an environment where they can be successful at their own developmental levels.

One of the primary reasons for this trend is the change of primary focus in education in these locations from the subject matter to the student and the needs of each child. Children develop at different rates, at different times, and in different ways. For some, the "light bulb" comes on regarding a given concept or idea at the "regular" time. Others take longer. Our traditional system of education has been very inflexible. Each student has had a set amount of time to "get it" or to fail. The multiage classroom gives students more time to develop, to grow, to get it, not unlike the one-room school of the past.

Educating the Whole Child

In the traditional setting, students have a set amount of time to learn and understand a set amount of information. The multiage classroom recognizes and, therefore, plans for a variety of pupil abilities, understands and provides for different rates of progress, and is flexible in the areas of social and emotional development (Lodish, 1992). This type of classroom is organized to include two or more age groups within one setting. Referring to children's ages, some examples of multiage classrooms might include the following:

5,6; 5,6,7; 5,6,7,8; 6,7,8 (*Transformations*, 1993)
8,9,10; 9,10,11 (Stone, 1994/1995)
6-12 (Aulgur, Baker, & Copeland, 1992)

The whole purpose in using this organization is to provide opportunities for interaction and cooperation between and among children who vary in age, experience, ability, and maturity (*Planbook*, 1995). Whatever the age grouping may be, the philosophy behind multiaging is to promote DAP to meet individual children's needs. DAP means providing curriculum and instruction that address the physical, social, intellectual, emotional, and aesthetic needs of young learners and permit a student to progress through an integrated curriculum at the student's own rate and pace. It is felt that a larger age span in grouping is more reflective of a child's environment outside of school where he or she interacts with a wide age range of individuals (Lodish, 1992).

A school with multiage classrooms does not use grade-level titles or designations for the students or the rooms involved in this type of grouping strategy (Pavan, 1992). If multiage grouping is used in only the primary grades, then classrooms may be designated Primary 1, Primary 2, and so on. Another technique is for the students and the teacher to decide on a class name at the beginning of the year, such as Mrs. Brown's Bears. Whatever method is adopted, it has been found that learning and the excitement about learning take place more smoothly when age and grade identifications disappear along with the constraints dictated by single-grade-level classrooms (Black, 1993).

In the multiage classroom, lots of things are happening differently. Children can help children (peer tutoring) without fear of being accused of cheating. Students get excited about learning because they do purposeful activities that are frequently hands-on. The children in a classroom become active participants in their own learning and help to collect materials and documentation for the evaluation and assessment of their own work (Pavan, 1992). Planning involves teachers and students. A variety of materials are in use, not just textbooks. Activities may be planned for whole group, small group, paired, or individual instruction. Students are excited about poetry, writing, math, and reading. Assessment is more authentic and casual and less threatening. Activity stations abound, and rows of desks are disappearing. Group and individual projects are filling the halls. Student work hangs everywhere in the classroom. A great deal of attention is directed toward the individual needs of each child. Teachers are facilitating and guiding, not directing all day. Children are once again becoming excited about learning!

This is all great, but can't this happen in single-grade classrooms? The answer is yes. But it won't be the same. There will still be real pressure on Johnny to pass. Writers won't be helping emergent writers. Readers won't be helping emergent readers. Brothers and sisters won't be helping siblings and "old" students won't be helping new students to become more familiar with a new environment and new processes. Children won't have the opportunity to learn and develop at their own rates without the ever-present concern about passing a given grade.

Why Return to the One-Room School Concept?

Why would we want to return to the one-room school, or at least to many of its characteristics? These ideas will help us to help children learn and like learning. Whether or not that was the original intent, the one-room school helped children learn at their own individual rate and be comfortable with that rate. An assignment, given to many levels, was evaluated at many levels, but accomplished by all. The process of students helping students in those days closely resembles the peer tutoring projects of today.

Teachers in multiage classrooms are amazed that something so simple as opening up the curriculum has attracted children back to learning who once were considered slow, lazy, problem children. Concepts are presented that would have been held for "the right grade level." Now the sky seems to be the limit when planning activities as long as DAP is maintained and students are evaluated according to their own potential and not compared to others (Stone, 1994/1995).

What Changes Will Be Needed?

A transition of this type does not take place overnight. It requires time, preparation, work, flexibility, and dedication. Individuals involved—teachers, students, parents, and administrators—will find that their roles will change. Each will take on new responsibilities to make the multiage classroom happen and be successful. The environment of the school, and the classroom in particular, will change dramatically. New materials will be required, some of which can be purchased and some that will need to be developed at the school level to meet individual needs of students. Who will make them? Everyone can help!

Activities and experiences planned for the children and the classroom will be different, more hands-on and active. Expectations will change as students relax and learn and as we find out that all children can learn, some in ways different than we provided in the traditional classroom. Probably the biggest change needed will be our own ideas as educators. For the multiage classroom to work, teachers must accept that they are going to learn a new way of teaching. Change can be exciting if we allow it to be so. Ready to forge ahead?

Planning for Multiage Instruction: The Teacher's Role

Currently, three states—Kentucky, Mississippi, and Oregon—have mandated multiage programs for young learners. In Kentucky, students who are or will be 5 years old by October 1 of the current school year are eligible to enter the Multiage/Multiability Primary Program. The primary program is defined as the first 4 years a child is in school. Within the primary program, each child progresses educationally at his or her own developmental rate and pace, with the teacher using continuous assessment to ensure individual progress and success. Students in the primary program do not fail, nor is there the need for them to skip a grade level to have an appropriate educational curriculum. When it is deemed to be in the child's best interest, he or she may spend a 5th year, or they may exit the program in fewer than 4 years.

Multiaging, as represented in Kentucky's primary programs, respects the wide range of developmental differences in young children. It allows children functioning below age group norms in some areas of their development to work with younger peers in a less stressful situation. At the opposite end of the spectrum, children who are functioning at above-age-norm levels may work with older or higher ability children at more challenging tasks. Teachers in a multiage setting usually are more accepting of developmental discrepancies among children than are teachers in single-grade settings. Uneven development in children is considered normal, and teachers plan for situations that can enhance children's motivation and self-confidence in the classroom.

In a traditional classroom representing a single grade, a teacher can depend on textbooks in the various disciplines to help plan the curriculum. The curriculum presented to children is often fragmented, with periods of time during the day set aside to study separate subjects. Many teachers in this setting become dispensers of information that has been predetermined to be appropriate for that age-graded level. But in a multiage class, what grade level would a teacher use? Let's take an example of a family grouping of children ages 5, 6, and 7. If the children began school for the year with these ages mixed in one classroom, the 7-year-old students would move to another family after 1 year with the teacher, and a new group of 5-year-olds would join. The original 6-year-olds would spend 2 years in the same family, and the 5-year-olds would be in the same family with the same teacher for 3 years.

If textbooks are not appropriate in a multiage classroom because their content is usually narrow and intended for one grade level only, then what is appropriate? Teaching in a multiage setting requires a paradigm shift for the teacher. He or she must move from the role of giver or dispenser of knowledge from textbooks to a curriculum developer and a facilitator for children's learning. But how can a teacher meet the individual needs of so many different-age learners?

Child-Centered Environments

Teachers in multiage classrooms understand that each child brings a different background of knowledge and experience with him or her to school. Therefore, children will take different paths in their attainment of knowledge and skills. Not only do children bring different levels of experience to the classroom, they also differ in their preferred learning style. Howard Gardner's (1985) book *Frames of Mind: The Theory of Multiple Intelligences* reminds us that individuals learn in various ways. Children can demonstrate their intelligence(s) through physical movement, music and rhythm, interpersonal relationships and communication, intrapersonal awareness, verbal and linguistic ability, scientific thinking, and visual and spatial coordination. Teachers of multiage children design authentic learning experiences that allow children to express their learning in multiple ways: reading, writing, speaking, listening, drawing, painting, singing, dancing, dramatizing, and constructing. This differs greatly from most traditional classrooms where children are required to express themselves mainly with paper-and-pencil tasks.

Changing Roles in the Multiage Classroom

Teachers in a multiage classroom must be trained for their new roles in the classroom. This training can be at the preservice or inservice level, but it will be critical for teachers' and students' success. Six key instructional dimensions have been identified from research that affect successful multigrade teaching: (a) instructional organization and curriculum planning, (b) classroom organization, (c) classroom management and discipline, (d) instructional delivery and grouping, (e) student self-directed learning, and (f) peer tutoring (Miller, 1991b). Each instructional dimension will be discussed in detail.

Instructional Organization and Curriculum Planning

In traditional graded classrooms, most teachers use the majority of their teaching day instructing their students in whole group situations. Reading is the one discipline that may be the exception. Traditionally, reading has been taught according to the child's reading ability level.

The teacher of multiage students must be prepared to meet the many learning levels and needs of the students. This can be achieved through teaching with an integrated curriculum approach. An integrated curriculum can be designed wherein teachers select a broad theme and organize every aspect of the curriculum around it. Organizing the curriculum around a theme can dissolve the barriers between subject areas and allow children of different ages and developmental stages to work together in a whole group, in a small group, with a peer, or individually. Many experienced teachers of multiage children consider the task of planning for an integrated curriculum one of the most difficult aspects of teaching in the multiage class.

Thematic study is one of the most commonly used strategies for integrating the curriculum. A broad theme can be thought of as a concept, such as patterns, change over time, human relationships, diversity, or physical wellness. This approach to curriculum development is much broader, will take a longer amount of time to investigate, and is more sophisticated than the typical unit an elementary teacher in the past may have planned. A broad-based theme versus a more narrow topical theme allows all discipline perspectives to focus on the theme. If a multiage teacher were to choose the narrow, short-term topical theme of "quilts," only a few disciplines could be correlated around the topical theme. For example, could the physical education teacher's curriculum be an integral part of the theme? (Daniel, 1994). What about the music curriculum, or the science curriculum? What higher level thinking can students expect to experience with the narrow theme of quilts? If, however, the teacher were to choose the broad theme of "patterns," everything within the young child's school day could be organized around the theme.

Thematic study refers to the core of what children do in the school. Teachers who want to use this strategy crisscross the curriculum, looking for natural connections. These connections may be among content areas, learning strategies, or instructional goals. The existing science or social studies curriculum is an area in which broad themes are evident and can be used to integrate all appropriate discipline content. The choice of a theme requires some considerations, such as whether the theme is broad enough to lend itself to comparing and contrasting and permit extensive investigation into concrete situations, materials, and resources. The broad theme must not be geographically or historically limiting, so that the surrounding world can be used as a laboratory for the study. Broad themes should encourage an understanding of and appreciation for the community. They are typically open-ended and encourage students to extend their investigations based on their individual interest (Bridge, 1994). If a subject area does not fit naturally into the thematic study, then that subject should be dealt with separately for the duration of the thematic study. Within the thematic study, teachers can also plan for the integration of the processes of reading, writing, listening, speaking, and thinking.

If we used the broad theme of patterns to design a thematic study, we could explore the theme from all aspects of the idea using the generalization that patterns repeat over and over; therefore, patterns help us guess what will happen next. There are patterns in music, art, literature, mathematics, science, social studies, creative arts, geometric shapes, culture, poetry, life cycles, space, daily routines, movements, and more. An example for a multiage class of lower elementary students ages 5, 6, and 7 could include literacy activities such as finding repeating patterns in children's literature in predictably patterned books and writing other versions of the stories they have read.

Children can find patterns in chants and rhymes and can compare the patterns found in different pieces of poetry. Poetry can be written following various patterns such as senryu, haiku, tanka, cinquain, limerick, and biopoem. In the area of mathematics, students can find number patterns on the calendar such as days, weeks, months, and years. Other number patterns used in the classroom can be identified. Children can use pattern or unit blocks to make and extend patterns. They may explore patterns in quilts, fabric, or wallpaper, noticing the changes in patterns as a result of rotations, slides, and flips. Students could explore patterns in measurement using water or sand and units of measure such as teaspoons, tablespoons, cups, pints, quarts, and gallons.

In the area of science, students can use a hand-held magnifying lens to observe patterns in fingerprints, leaves, tree rings, and spider webs. Students can look for patterns of legs and body parts in identifying insects. An investigation of patterns in seasonal change could be conducted that includes the plant life cycle, the food chain, or the water cycle. In the area of creative arts, students could create and extend patterns with sponge printing, using collage materials and textile scraps. Children can find patterns in simple dance steps and physical activities such as marching and skipping. There are patterns in musical scales, in repeating musical phrases, and in clapping the rhythms in children's names.

In the area of social studies, students can find street patterns on maps of their communities or city. They can investigate patterns in bus, trolley, or train routes, if appropriate. They could investigate patterns of children's families within their classroom, for example, the number of siblings or pets. Students can graph patterns regarding how many parents work and what type of work they do.

Indeed, the broad theme of patterns would need to have some limits set and a sequence and purpose of study developed. Teachers can do this by writing one or more essential or guiding questions. An essential question can be defined as a question that guides or focuses students' attention to critical theme outcomes and encourages higher level and critical thinking.

Some considerations must be made before choosing a broad theme and writing essential or guiding questions. One must consider not only the principles of developmental appropriateness for children but also the educational appropriateness of the theme and the learning station activities. The following questions can help the teacher judge the educational appropriateness of broad themes:

- Is the concept being considered worth knowing by young children?
- Are there situations where it will be useful to them?
- Will knowing this concept help children participate in and contribute to their society in some meaningful way? (Gatzke, 1991, p. 101)

If the teacher has determined that the broad theme is developmentally and educationally appropriate, then the essential questions for the thematic study can be written. Some considerations include the following:

1. The questions should be written so every person in the class can understand them.
2. The questions should be open-ended, with no obvious "right" answer.

3. The questions should reflect higher order thinking. They should require synthesis, analysis, and evaluation or judgment.
4. They should be personalized to generate greater personal student interest and allow students to be more creative.
5. There should be a logical sequence to the questions.
6. The questions should emphasize concepts while requiring students to use knowledge in developing answers.
7. They should be posted in the classroom and shared with parents in class newsletters or notes home (*Transformations*, 1993).

Using the example of patterns and a multiage class of students aged 5, 6, and 7, we might write a series of essential questions:

- What is a pattern, and what are some patterns I can create and extend? (This question is basic to the understanding of patterns.)
- What are some patterns I can observe in my everyday life?
- How do patterns affect my everyday life?
- What are some ways I can use the study of patterns to understand and interpret past and present events?
- Using the study of patterns, what are some future predictions I can make?

Another strategy teachers can use to generate essential questions is to involve the students in the planning process. A know/want/learned (KWL) process could be used with the entire class in a brainstorming and charting activity. What do I know about patterns? What do I want to know about patterns? At the conclusion of the thematic study on patterns, students could review and reflect on their learning by brainstorming and charting the answer to the question, "What did I learn about patterns?"

Broad thematic studies use teaching and learning approaches from current best practices for young learners. These include the following:

- A whole language approach to reading in which meaning rather than just phonics or word recognition is central.

- A process approach to writing.
- A problem-solving approach to math through the use of concrete materials.
- A discovery approach to science and social studies.

Broad themes allow the teacher to focus on a topic of interest to the students and work toward desired outcomes in various content areas. Broad thematic studies are not peripheral to the curriculum, but integral. They lend themselves to teaching children of different ages, backgrounds, and ability in one setting. As knowledge and skills of students accumulate and develop, the work can grow in depth, complexity, and sophistication (Katz and Chard, 1989).

Classroom Organization

The physical environment of a primary classroom with multiage students must be carefully planned. The environment must provide space for students to work together in small groups (the workplace), room for an entire class meeting (a "gathering place"), and an area in which a child can work alone. There must be areas for quiet activities and for more active situations. In this environment, each child does not have to be assigned an individual desk or a seat at a table, but can work within the shared space of the classroom. When all students need to meet together for the thematic lesson, or for an entire class activity, the gathering place can be used. The ideal multiage classroom is planned with the many activities that will take place kept in mind and is arranged with learning stations or centers in the room where children can work in small groups or independently.

A learning station can be defined as any focal point or area within a classroom that contains activities and/or materials used to educate, reinforce, and enrich a skill or learning concept. Learning stations do not imply that learning will take place only in that area of the room, but are specific locations where related materials are arranged for children's independent use in the classroom. These learning stations allow children to construct knowledge independently from interactions with materials as well as cooperatively with other children. Learning stations contain hands-on experimentation and exploration activities for children. The teacher should plan an environment in which children can move and talk and be autonomous, self-directed, and responsible learners.

Why Learning Stations Are Effective

Teachers of multiage children report that learning stations or learning centers are an effective teaching strategy for the following reasons:

- Centers promote active student involvement.
- Centers allow students to move at their own rates and at their own levels of ability.
- Centers provide students with opportunities to make choices.
- Centers are flexible; they provide opportunities for students to work independently or cooperatively with other students.
- Centers are compatible with thematic studies. (Bridge, 1994)

Planning the Physical Environment for Learning Stations

When planning for learning stations, first consider the many types of activities that go on in a multiage classroom. Few classrooms will be large enough for each learning activity to have its own space, so the room space must be designed to accommodate multiple uses. Before arranging the furniture in the classroom, one must consider the location of the doors, windows, chalkboards, bulletin boards, heating and cooling units, and electrical outlets. Traffic-flow patterns must be analyzed, especially high-traffic areas around doors, restrooms, and water fountains, which should have pathways for easy access. Children should be able to move around the room without having to walk through learning stations and disturb students who are working there. Picture a square classroom, visually divide the room, and plan an area for quieter activities that includes the library, computer(s), language arts, a writing table, and perhaps a listening station. Another area could be designated for more active involvement such as block building, woodworking, dramatic role-playing, or music-making. An area for messy or wet activities (e.g., art or science projects) is needed, and a water table could be considered. The room should have an area for whole class meeting (the gathering place), which needs to be located near an electrical outlet for a record player, tape player, TV/VCR, and so on.

Each area of the room will need to be planned so that all materials to be used by the students are accessible. Also consider labeling the learning station areas and posting student directions for use in each area. This labeling strategy will help encourage students to be self-directed learners and will help enforce following and interpreting directions. Materials can be stored on low, open shelving, which can be labeled, under clear plastic, with words or a picture of the material that belongs on the shelf. This labeling of shelves encourages children to be independent in getting needed materials for themselves and aids in the cleanup process by allowing students to know where materials belong. Shelving units can be used to section off the area to control the classroom traffic, as well as form a small, well-defined and enclosed work area that provides young children with a sense of security and encourages them to stay on task.

The type of work the children will be undertaking in the learning station will determine if a rug area is needed for students to work on the floor, or if a table area is more appropriate. As in all primary or lower elementary classrooms, the children's furniture will need to be the appropriate size for the students and, of course, in good repair.

When assessing the learning environment in a primary multiage class, the teacher may consider the following questions:

1. Can a child or small group get materials (paper, markers, pencils, scissors, etc.) and find a comfortable place to work?
2. Is it possible for students to move around the room without disturbing the work of others?
3. Is there a quiet place for a child or small group of children to read or think?
4. Does the furniture arrangement allow moving from a whole or large group situation to small group or individual

instruction without major disruptions to the classroom routine? (Brewer, 1995)

In addition, while planning the physical layout of the room, teachers will want to provide a space for students to store their personal items and hang their coats. Space will also be needed to display student work. Teachers will need to plan for storage of items that are currently not in use, as well as for consumable items such as construction and art paper, large containers of glue, and paint.

Designing Learning Stations

For children to work in a small group or individually in the learning stations, they must understand what their role for behavior and involvement is in this environment. Also, the learning stations must be designed to support the child's need for independence.

All learning stations must have the following components:

1. *Directions.* All directions in the learning station and on learning activities should be simple and clearly stated; they may be written or tape recorded.
2. *Purpose.* The purpose of the station should be obvious. The students must understand not only what the station is for but also what is expected of them while they are participating at the station.
3. *Content.* This is why the station exists. The learning station can include manipulative materials, media, books, other people, and so on to communicate the content.
4. *Activities.* There should be a variety of developmental levels of activities and multiple ways the students can apply what they have learned in the learning station.

Learning stations in the classroom may be described as either permanent or temporary. Permanent learning stations are those that remain for a long time, possibly even the entire school year, although the activities in the stations may change according to the teacher's goals and objectives for the students in the class. Temporary learning stations refer to the activities that relate to the current thematic study being investigated.

Examples of permanent learning stations may include Library, Reading, Listening, Creative Writing, the Post Office or Message Station, Spelling, Handwriting, Mathematics, Science and Exploration, Social Studies, Blocks, Dramatic Play, Art, Music, Table Games, and Construction, and a sand-and-water table area. A rotating gallery approach to displaying students' written and drawn work throughout the classroom would be appropriate. Teachers can consider a Literacy learning station, which combines the Computer station with the traditional Library, Writing, and Listening stations. The focus of this station would be on meaning making, where children would be encouraged to create their own texts using paper and pencil, tape recorders, or the computer. Regardless of what the learning station is called, when appropriate activities are provided for students, they will have the opportunity to learn at their own rates and levels of complexity.

The Teacher's Role With Learning Stations

The teacher has four major roles to fulfill when using learning stations.

The Preparer of the Station. This involves planning the activities that are developmentally and educationally appropriate and related to the theme under investigation. All necessary equipment and learning tools must be gathered. The tasks should be as close to real life as possible.

The Introducer. Students must know what is expected at each station. How is the task to be undertaken, the game played, or the activity completed? Where are the materials that are necessary for the activity located? Where are students to put their finished products? This introduction to the learning station can be accomplished by introducing the station to the entire class during the "gathering" time or to a small group of students during the small group work time during the day. This small group of students (three to seven students) can then teach other students how to do the activity or task.

The Encourager. Materials and activities in the learning stations need to be changed to keep children from growing bored. New materials and fresh creative activities will encourage students to be on task and producing at their highest ability. The teacher might encourage the students to create activities such as board games or crossword puzzles that can be included in the learning station. Be sure to share individual student products and pieces of work with the entire class. This encourages children to produce quality work and increases the children's self-esteem.

The Accounter. Evaluation can be very simple, using teacher-developed checklists or a more involved process. The evaluation should be centered on the growth of the students in using learning station materials independently and their ability to work cooperatively with other children. Anecdotal notes can be written on the students' progress by the teacher. In addition, children's self-reflection or their thoughts about their work in the learning station can be recorded. Students can share what they have learned, what was difficult or interesting, or what their favorite aspect of an activity was. This form of assessment requires the child to use metacognition and informs the teacher on the children's progress. Student reflection can also serve as an evaluation of the learning station's effectiveness. All forms of evaluation can be shared with students and their parents.

If the task of planning for active child involvement in the multiage classroom by developing learning stations seems overwhelming to you, you are not alone. Experienced teachers in multiage classrooms suggest beginning with learning stations that are easier to develop and planning initial activities for a Library station, a Computer station, and a Writing station. As teachers and students become comfortable with the management and movement within the classroom, more learning stations can be added.

Classroom Management and Discipline

Managing the multiage classroom, including student discipline, is another instructional dimension area that must be carefully thought through when planning. We have investigated the need for multiage grouping with young children and the need for an integrated approach to the curriculum to meet the uneven developmental needs of multiage learners. Because learning stations, cooperative learning, and whole language approaches encourage students to choose and move about the classroom somewhat freely, classroom management strategies appropriate for a multiage class must be employed. Now we will explore the task of managing this active learning environment.

Research tells us that when student diversity increases, whether the setting is a traditional, graded classroom or a multiage classroom, greater demand is placed on teacher resources, "both cognitive and emotional" (Miller, 1991b). Successful teaching in a multiage classroom will depend on the teacher's ability to plan classroom schedules and routines that promote clear, predictable instructional patterns, especially those that enhance students' responsibility for their own learning (Miller, 1991b).

Any teaching situation demands that three important student behaviors be taught in the first days of school. These are discipline, procedures, and routines. These three behaviors become critical in the multiage classroom where children must be able to work cooperatively with other students as well as alone.

Establishing Rules

In any classroom, a discipline plan is needed that will help minimize classroom disturbances and maximize learning (Wong, 1991). The teacher must have a clear idea of what is expected from students, and the students must know what the teacher expects from them. Prior to the first day of school, the teacher should think through what expectations for student behavior will be. On the first day of school, one of the tasks that must be accomplished is for the students and the teacher to establish the classroom rules. This can be done while all the students are in the gathering place with the teacher. Our experience has been that even very young children can be guided into making a few (no more than five) appropriate class rules. The students can brainstorm all the rules they think will be necessary; at this time the teacher will accept and record all of the suggestions. The list can be narrowed and rules combined after the initial brainstorming activity. Remember to concentrate on the positive during the final revising of the list. Make the rules reflect positive behavior such as "Do walk" instead of "Don't run." The final list of class rules can then be posted in the room. When children are involved in the rule-making process, they are more likely to see the need to follow the rules. Self-sufficiency and self-direction of students within this environment are valued, and rules are treated as a responsibility that is necessary for running the class. When misbehavior does occur, the teacher can work with the individual child or a small group of children, reminding the students of the rule they helped create that was broken and discussing what the correct behavior should be.

Teaching Procedures

Many classroom problems arise when students have not been taught classroom procedures. This can be a problem in any classroom, but it is critical in a multiage classroom. Multiage classrooms contain many diverse student learning levels and styles, and the classroom's physical environment encourages active student involvement, making the teaching of procedures essential. Classroom procedures are necessary for several reasons, as follows:

- Classroom procedures are statements of expectations necessary for students to participate in the classroom activities and to learn.
- Classroom procedures allow many varied activities to take place with a minimum of confusion and wasted instructional time.
- Classroom procedures allow students to know how things are to operate in the classroom, and help them to figure out what the teacher wants. Children want to know the rules and limits for their behavior and are more secure in an environment where the rules and procedures are clear and consistently enforced. (Wong, 1991)

Teachers in multiage classrooms must plan for every aspect of their day and teach the correct behaviors to and model them for the students. A three-step approach to teaching procedures can be used. First, explain the procedure and demonstrate and model the correct way to do the procedure. Second, have children rehearse the procedure. Third, reinforce the procedure throughout the school day and year as needed. The following are examples of the necessary procedures that need consideration:

- Emergency procedures, fire drills, and so forth (How are students to respond when they hear an emergency alert?)
- What students are to do when they enter the classroom
- What you will do when you want the group's attention
- How transitions between activities will be handled
- Student procedures for locating additional materials, paper, pencils, and so on
- Student movement within the classroom
- What students are to do with completed work from the learning stations
- How learning station rotations will be handled
- Cleanup procedures after students finish working in the learning stations
- What students are to do if they finish their tasks early
- What a student with a question or needing the teacher's help should do
- How restroom and water breaks will be handled
- Student behavior in regard to voice loudness levels within the various learning stations

A great deal of time will be spent at the beginning of the school year introducing, teaching, modeling, and rehearsing procedures. All procedures will not be learned in a day, but this aspect of classroom management will be critical for students if they are to learn to be self-sufficient and able to work independently in the multiage active classroom environment.

Practiced Procedures Can Become Student Routines

Procedures can be reinforced by reminding students of the way the correct procedure is to be performed. Using the class procedure of requiring students to raise their hands to be called on before speaking when they are in the gathering place as an example, the teacher can remind students of the procedure if students begin calling out their responses. "Students, remember you must raise your hand and be called on before giving an answer." As students begin to raise their hands, the teacher can say, "I'm going to call on Courtney because she remembered to raise her hand and wait to be called on." In other circumstances when a more complicated procedure is involved, the teacher may have the few students not doing the procedure correctly practice and experience the correct way to do the procedure. Young children respond very well to positive reinforcement for their correct behavior. Specific praise can go a long way in encouraging correct behavior in any classroom. Planning for, explaining, rehearsing, and using positive reinforcement can help children learn classroom procedures so that they become student routines within the school day. The goal of student routines is for students to know what is expected of them and to make correct choices for their own behavior.

Let's review what is planned for students in a developmentally appropriate multiage classroom. Teachers have designed an integrated curriculum around a broad theme that allows students to compare, contrast, and investigate a topic of interest to them. Learning stations that have interesting activities and that contain hands-on experimentation and exploration activities for children have been developed. Classroom rules, with input from the students, have been developed. Procedures have been taught, reviewed, and practiced by students until they become routine. In this active, child-centered environment where respect for each individual is expected and practiced, behavior problems can still arise. As problems arise, teachers will thoughtfully and calmly work with each child and the child's parent(s), when necessary, to solve the problem.

Instructional Delivery and Grouping

Instructional grouping practices play an important role in an effective multigrade/multiage classroom. The teacher emphasizes the similarities among the different grades and ages and teaches to them, thus conserving valuable teaching time (Miller, 1991b). Instruction in the multiage class will be a combination of whole group and small group instruction and individual instruction when necessary. Children will be grouped in flexible groups that are regrouped throughout the day. These groups are based on student-demonstrated needs and abilities, not on IQ or previous performance.

Whole group instruction can be used when teaching a concept related to the thematic study or in a situation where there is an open-task activity to be introduced to all of the students. If a writing assignment related to the thematic study is assigned, all students can participate in a prewriting brainstorming activity. This whole group activity will allow all students to discuss the topic from a different perspective and will help all students learn to respect the opinions of others. During the time that students are actually writing, the teacher can schedule individual writing conferences with students. When it is necessary, a group of students who are making similar writing mistakes can be pulled into a group for a skills lesson. The difference between a multiage developmentally appropriate whole group lesson and a whole group lesson in a traditional classroom is that in a multiage classroom, only content that all students need or can use is taught to the whole group. Any instruction that is skills related and that only certain students need is taught in a temporary small group or individual situation. This difference in grouping for instruction is developmentally appropriate because each student is able to work at his or her individual rate and pace. Children who are familiar with the skill being introduced are not bored, and children who are not yet ready are not frustrated. This grouping and regrouping will allow children of different ages and abilities, boys and girls, to interact with children of different backgrounds, personalities, interests, and abilities. These groupings reflect the realities of daily living (Burruss, 1993).

The following groupings are appropriate for any child:

- *Problem solving.* In this grouping, learners are grouped around a common unsolved problem or topic, such as a science experiment.
- *Instructional needs.* Students are grouped for instruction in a concept or skill.
- *Reinforcement.* Learners who need more practice or need reteaching in a specific area or task are grouped together.

- *Interest.* Students who are working on a common self-selected activity are grouped to work together.
- *Multiple intelligences.* Students are grouped and regrouped according to their identified multiple intelligence strengths and/or areas for growth.
- *Peer tutoring.* Children can learn from one another by giving and receiving help.
- *Cooperative learning.* Children can be grouped to participate in a clearly designed and assigned task. This grouping would require the students to be instructed in cooperative learning strategies. The students work collaboratively with all participants, but each is held individually accountable for academic performance and social behavior.
- *Book share talks.* Five students a day or week, on a rotating basis, give an overview (or a portion if it is a chaptered book) of the book they will read orally to the group and lead a discussion on. Students not leading the book share choose the book they wish to hear and form a group. The book promoter then reads and asks students in the group questions they have prepared related to the book. A self-evaluation or reflection sheet can be used by the book promoter regarding his or her own reading fluency, ability to conduct the group, and so on. (*Primary Your Way*, 1995)

To effectively group students, teachers must be aware of individual student needs. This will require teachers to use assessment practices that are developmentally appropriate.

Assessment can be defined as the process of observing, recording, and documenting the work that children do and how they do it, as the basis for educational decisions that affect those children. This type of assessment should be viewed as ongoing and a natural part of everyday instruction. It is intended to help develop an accurate profile of student growth and help with instructional decisions teachers must make. Assessment should be child centered and classroom based and should emphasize a student's strengths.

Teacher observation is an important tool to use for assessment. Teachers observe how children learn and interact with one another, and then interpret what has been observed. This information can be used to plan effectively for instructional strategies, student groupings, and students' continuous progress in the multiage class. There are a number of authentic assessment measurement strategies that teachers can use to profile student growth.

Anecdotal records are brief, positive narrative accounts of a child's progress based on milestones particular to that child. They can include social, emotional, physical, aesthetic, and cognitive development. The recordings are made when appropriate throughout the day. An example might be, "Jordan read the book *Brown Bear, Brown Bear, What Do You See?* orally today during reading conference without any errors" (include the date of the conference).

Work samples are examples of children's work that have been saved to record the child's progress. These may include writing samples or art work over time—anything that is perceived as significant.

Checklists of behaviors, instructional objectives, or skills are arranged in a logical order. As children are observed, the presence or absence of the behavior or skill can be noted. By analyzing the checklist, teachers can verify their observations without having to rely on memory.

An assessment portfolio is a collection of a child's work that demonstrates the child's efforts, progress, and achievement over time. The accumulation of work in the portfolio involves the child and the teacher as they discuss which materials should be included that best reflect the student's learning.

Authentic forms of assessment can inform teachers of student's progress and aid in instructional strategies planning. All forms of assessment can also be used as a starting point for parent-teacher conversations about student progress.

Student Self-Directed Learning

From the first day students enter a multiage classroom, they must have the opportunity to learn how they can help themselves and others in the class. The climate in the classroom is one wherein children are collaborators in their own learning and learn from each other as well as from the teacher. Many teachers use the classroom saying "Ask three before you ask me." This means check with three other students for a solution to your problem or question before you ask the teacher. This approach to self-directed learning reinforces for children the idea that they do not have to be dependent on adults as the only source of knowledge and for answers to all their questions. It encourages students to seek information from their peers and other sources.

Every aspect of planning in the multiage classroom is geared toward strategies that teach and encourage students toward a high level of independence. Strategies, such as thematic studies, that encourage content integration and motivate students to investigate interesting ideas from multiple perspectives help young children learn more efficiently. Learning stations that allow students to make choices in their selection of activities encourage student self-direction. A clear management and discipline system that enhances students' responsibility for their own behavior and learning is employed in effective multiage classrooms. And developmentally appropriate teaching strategies are always used by teachers. These aspects and strategies help direct young children toward independence, self-reliance, and lifelong self-directed learning.

Peer Tutoring

Children can gain an increased sense of social competence when they are able to establish productive social and working relationships with other children. The teaching strategy of peer tutoring can be taught by adults and then coached as children use the strategy with each other. Peer tutoring can be defined as the "one-to-one teaching process in which the tutor is one of the same general academic status as the tutee" (Cohen, 1986, p. 175). Peer tutoring is a strategy that works well in a multiage class as children who have mastered content and processes can help other children who are still in the beginning learning stages. This natural strategy has been used for years by students who understand the lesson and try to help their peers who do not. In fact, when many of us were in school it might have been called cheating. This tutoring can have positive effects on both the tutor and the tutee. The tutor has the opportunity to be a teacher or leader within the class as well as a learner or follower. This can lead to an increased sense of self-confidence. The peer tutoring situation also has positive effects for young learners who learn well with individualized instruction. A child's learning experience may also be less stressful when the teaching comes from another child who may be more sensitive to the child than an adult might be.

Strong evidence exists that students at all levels of achievement can be effective tutors, but teachers will want to be careful in using this strategy. Students should not be asked to tutor frequently. This technique is not intended to create a few students as "junior teachers" on a daily basis.

Peer tutoring can take several forms in the multiage classroom. Besides being used to help a child grasp a concept or solve a problem, it can be used to refine or check work. When teaching students the "Writing Process," the following steps can be taught to all students for asking another student for a peer conference during the revising stage:

- Politely ask a peer to conference with you (the author).
- The author will read his or her writing to the peer.
- The author will ask the peer what the peer thinks about what the author read to him or her.
- Next, the peer will read the writing.
- After the peer finishes reading, the author will ask if he or she has any questions.
- The next step involves the first stages of editing: The author asks if the peer has any suggestions for correct spelling, punctuation, and so on.
- During the last step, the peer gives the author a positive comment about his or her work.

This form of peer tutoring can allow a younger child, as well as an older one, to be "the teacher."

Elements of peer tutoring are found in cooperative learning, an instructional method in which students are heterogeneously grouped to produce academic and social gains. Students are individually accountable for their learning, yet also experience a sense of interdependency for the success of their group.

The extensive research on cooperative learning suggests that it is the cooperative aspect that is most effective in enhancing student achievement. Students' motivation is increased when they work in a cooperative learning group. Cooperation is necessary in a multiage class as well as in life.

Effective teaching in a multiage class will require teachers who understand child development and developmentally appropriate practice, who can plan integrated curricula, and who can plan a classroom environment that encourages active child involvement. Teachers in this environment will need well-developed organizational and management skills. Additional planning time will be required if teachers are to use continuous student progress so all students are working at their own ability level. Indeed, teaching in the multiage class will be demanding, and extensive preparation will be necessary.

$$\diamondsuit\ 3\ \diamondsuit$$

Inside a Multiage Classroom:
The Physical Arrangement

Welcome to a classroom that is planned exclusively for the learning success of multiage young children. Even before the door to the classroom is opened, you know you are in a special place. Outside the room in the hallway, student work is displayed— art, writing, poetry, science reports, and mathematical word problems that have multiple solutions and are attractively arranged. On the door, there is a large cardboard tree where children's names are printed on the green leaves and "Welcome to Our Family" is printed above.

Inside, you may be amazed at the physical layout of the room. Instead of rows of student desks and a teacher's desk in the front of the room, you see tables and chairs. Areas of the room are divided into small, interesting-looking work areas. Classroom furniture includes a couch, a rocking chair, bean bag chairs, and individual desks in a quiet area. This classroom literally invites children to learn by providing comfortable places to work and read. An aquarium, a terrarium, a classroom library, a puppet stage, a book production center, and computers are also in the classroom. Children's work, drawings, and projects are attractively displayed throughout the room. This classroom is equipped and arranged to provide challenging opportunities for all children to work and learn.

The Library station has an area rug on the floor, bean bag chairs, large pillows, and even an old bathtub on legs that has been fitted with a pad to provide a soft, cozy spot to read. A library rack is filled with reading materials: a wide assortment of trade books, picture books, chaptered books, fiction and nonfiction books, books that reflect the thematic study of "patterns," children's magazines, and even a recent local newspaper. This area also includes copies of books written and illustrated by individual students and the whole class.

Close by, there are individual Listening stations equipped with student headphones. A wide variety of listening materials is available, classical music as well as stories on tape. Some of the story tapes are commercially produced, and others have been made by the teacher, parents, older students from other classes, and students in the class. One tape you decide to listen to is titled *Tuesday* by "Wesley." The story is a take-off on the wordless picture book *Tuesday* by David Wiesner. Wesley, a nonreader, has told the story by "reading" the pictures.

The next area you investigate is the Writing station. This area includes reference materials, pictures, a chart of the class members' names, a computer, and a printer. A wide variety of writing and illustrating materials and many types of paper—lined, unlined, construction, colored, and stationery—and envelopes are located on a low shelf. There is a table in this area with six chairs. Here, children can use the "Writing Process" to develop stories and work through the entire book production process. They can write letters and notes to fellow classmates, family members, and friends. In this area, the emphasis is on communication, and students are encouraged to write to express themselves in many different ways. As you read some of the stories that are in the revising stage, you realize that the students are encouraged to use developmental or "best guess" spelling. The emphasis now is placed on students getting their thoughts on paper; correcting grammar and spelling errors will be dealt with before the piece "goes public." Within this area, there are wall charts with frequently used words that relate to the thematic study for student reference. Quick Spell handbooks and dictionaries are in the reference area. Several stories are in the editing stage where students correct their spelling and writing errors before the stories are "published."

Within this area of the room, there is also a Message Station that has 6-inch-square mailboxes. The mailboxes are labeled with each child's name as well as the name of each adult who works in the room. Children and adults can leave correspondence for each other in this area.

Three computers are grouped in this area of the room. These computers are used for tutorials, drill and practice, and simulations. A clipboard is used to sign up for computer time, and a timer reminds students when their allotted time is over.

Another learning area is the Art station. This station invites children to express themselves creatively. The equipment may include an easel, a drying rack, various kinds of art paper, paint, crayons, chalk, markers, scissors, glue, clay, and boxes that contain material for designing collages, such as scraps (e.g., fabric, yarn, or ribbon), buttons, dried beans, dried pasta, wrapping paper, tissue paper, and old greeting cards. These materials are located on low shelves. Each item has a place on the shelf, labeled with its picture and name and covered with clear plastic. The floor in this area is protected by heavy plastic, which is taped down. There is a table with four chairs. A stack of old newspapers is near, ready to be used to cover the table when messy projects are planned. This area is next to the sink, and soap and towels are close by for quick cleanups. Smocks to cover children's clothes hang on a rack.

An Exploration and Science learning station is also located in this area of the room, along with the class aquarium and terrarium. Activities are related to the biological, physical, and earth sciences. Unlike some science stations in traditional classrooms that look like a "shrine to science," with the obligatory plant, seashell, rock, and pinecone, this station has material for children to observe and classify and about which they can make predictions. Science experiments are written using a rebus approach. There are few words, and many steps in the directions are pictures that allow even beginning readers to conduct simple experiments. All children working in this station are encouraged to think and act like scientists. The emphasis is on the student being actively involved.

A note to adults is posted informing them of the potential for learning that this station offers. The note informs the reader that throughout the year(s), students will have the opportunity to

- Gather facts by means of direct observation
- Interpret and organize data
- Measure and record findings
- Speculate and make hypotheses
- Use new tools and techniques
- Clarify problems
- Report findings accurately

A small Construction station is located near the Art and Science stations. The equipment includes a workbench, hammer, saw, screwdriver, small roofing nails, screws, scraps of lumber, and safety goggles. A list of safety rules is posted along with a reminder that only two students may work in this area at a time.

The Dramatics station is housed in the area with the puppet stage. Here, there are large storage boxes labeled with their contents: "Uniforms," "Hats," "Shoes," "Dress-up," and "Accessories." This is an area where students can role-play themselves or use puppets to act out roles, or perhaps write a play in the Writing station and design puppets to act out the parts in the Art station.

The Mathematics station is where manipulatives are stored. Some of the materials included in this area are pattern blocks, bear counters, geo-boards, unifix cubes, base ten rods, attribute blocks, measuring materials, rulers, measuring tapes, a simple balance, and a scale. Task cards with math activities are included along with simple open-response questions that require critical thinking and computation to solve. There is an area rug that invites students to sit on the floor, as well as a table and chairs. A Puzzle and Game station adjoins the math center and the work space can be shared.

A total of 12 learning stations are set up within the classroom. Activities in one station frequently can be combined with those in another station. All stations are equipped with the necessary consumable materials, paper, pencils, reference materials, books, and media equipment.

A large space is provided in the front of the room near the whiteboard. The electrical outlet is in this area. There is a television, a VCR, and a tape recorder/player.

On an area of the whiteboard, there is a large space for the calendar and weather chart. There are cardboard dolls labeled "Today," "Yesterday," and "Tomorrow"; a "Days in School" timeline; and an "Incredible Equations" chart.

Children are beginning to arrive. The teacher has told you she will explain her daily schedule and discuss some of the activities the children are working on during the time the children are scheduled to work in the learning stations. You are invited to visit the Parent Corner and review the materials that are available to check out for home use.

As children enter the room, you decide to watch one student as she goes about her morning routine. You choose Courtney because she has her name on her jacket. Courtney hangs up her jacket, puts her backpack in her cubby space, and proceeds to the sign-in area. Here she moves her Velcro-backed name tag to the area of the tagboard labeled "Plate Lunch." The other side of the board is for students who have brought a packed lunch from home. Name tags not moved to either area would indicate that the child is absent. This morning routine allows the teacher to quickly prepare the lunch report for the cafeteria and the attendance report for the school office.

Courtney proceeds to the "Classroom Morning Announcements" board. Here some tasks are written in red marker and others in blue. The key at the bottom of the board gives the legend. Activities written in red are to be completed before the principal makes the morning announcements, and those in blue are to be completed after the announcements but no later than 8:45 a.m. Every morning when children enter the classroom, they have an activity to complete. The activities vary day by day as to type and content. This strategy gives children a purpose when they enter the room and encourages them to begin work on their own without waiting for an adult to tell them it is time to begin. It also allows for the staggered arrival of students. Children are busy with a meaningful task and time is not wasted waiting for everyone to arrive.

On finishing her "red" activity, Courtney moves from the table where she was working to the bulletin board area to look at the "Brag Squares." This board is divided into 12-inch squares, with a student's name on each square. Students may display any type of work or drawing they choose in their Brag Square, and the item on display may be changed daily. Among the items on display are drawings, journal entries, book drafts, reading and writing responses logs, stories, and poems. This area is a favorite among students, parents, and classroom visitors.

The morning arrival routine allows children time to perform classroom chores, which are assigned on a rotating basis. Students take care of the classroom fish and two gerbils and water the plants once a week. During this time, students may observe the progress of any projects taking place in the learning stations or they may choose to do recreational reading.

As soon as the morning announcements begin, all students are to come to the gathering place for the pledge to the flag and any school announcements. During this time, there is a brief "good morning" welcome made by the teacher, and any necessary additional class announcements are made. Students then return to various areas in the classroom with their journals and a clipboard to complete the morning's "blue" assignment, a writing prompt: "What morning routine pattern were you able to observe before your arrival at school?" Courtney chooses to work in the reading area, which has a rug, bean bag chairs, and many soft pillows. All children are allowed to work in the environment in which they are most comfortable. Some choose to sit at a table, others on the floor, some on the couch. At 8:45 a.m., all children return to the gathering place with their work.

During this time, the writing prompt is discussed and the teacher writes the children's responses on the whiteboard. Some of the observed morning patterns include wake-up time, morning routine of breakfast, grooming and dressing for school, and routines of required chores before school such as bed making. The route the school bus takes each morning to pick up children for school is suggested as a pattern. The writing prompt serves as a lead-in to the thematic study, a whole group mini-lesson on patterns. The lesson is well planned, and the students are engaged.

Questions are thoughtfully asked, and the student answers receive respectful responses from the teacher.

Music is used at this time to allow the children a change of pace from their work time. They sing a song and use creative movement to accompany it. Because it was fun, the children ask to repeat it.

The whole-group time is followed by an hour at the learning stations. Students are dismissed from the gathering place by the teacher, who says, "If you have on red shoes you may get your learning station folder, if you have on white shoes . . ." Children walk to the shelf to get their folders. Because it is still early in the school year, the teacher has chosen to use learning station contracts with the students. The learning stations are coded with simple symbols, and the activities in the stations are color coded as to their level of difficulty.

Children in this class quickly find the area they are to work in today and settle in to read their individual contracts. The teacher is circulating through the room ready to answer questions if the students need additional help. Another teacher has arrived in the classroom and is at the Reading station with the students there. When the students have settled down to work, it is your time to find out more about teaching in this type of active environment.

Your immediate questions for the teacher are about what you have observed so far. *Why are contracts used for the learning stations?* The teacher responds that contracts at the beginning of the school year are a management tool. As students become more accustomed to making choices, they can be phased out. Now they are required to work in four stations during the week and complete activities that are theme related. After they complete the required activities, there is a "Choose a Station" contract that the student may fill out. If a student finishes working in one station, he or she may go to another station if time permits and if there is room for the student in the station. In some of the stations, the number of students who may participate is controlled by the number of chairs at the table. In other stations, a picture with a specific number of children is posted. This lets students know how many children are allowed in the station at a time. For example, only two children may work in the Construction station at a time. The area is small, there are a limited number of tools, and the work the students are doing requires that an adult be near to ensure that the children are following the safety rules.

As the year progresses, teacher and student choice can be used for learning station selection, but for now the contracts lend a sense of security. Every child in the class can be evaluated by the completed contract and the product(s) he or she produces. The contract can also be shared with parents. Many parents who are new to the multiage class sometimes are skeptical that their child can actually be learning when they are having a good time, so the contract and product can be reassuring. If you take a close look and listen to the children, you realize that it may look like play but the children are also working and learning. Children learn best when they can experience the learning in a real-life, hands-on situation.

How do you fit in all of the subjects that children need to know? Do you teach basic skills? Throughout the day, large blocks of time are scheduled for activities such as the work now going on in the learning stations. Activities are planned that require active child involvement, interaction, and when possible, exploration and discovery. The curriculum is designed around broad themes such as the one they are working on now: patterns. A whole language approach is used to teach the basic skills of reading, listening, speaking, and writing, which are taught as a whole throughout the curriculum and the day, not as fragmented skills. Children are taught the "Writing Process," and writing-across-the-curriculum activities are implemented. Skills are taught, but not in the same way they might be in a more traditional classroom. The students also use manipulatives, multisensory materials, and technology every day.

There is another teacher with students in the Reading station. What is her role in the classroom? In this class there are students who have diverse learning needs. Mrs. Evans is the Special Education teacher. The two teachers work in collaboration, and Mrs. Evans comes in during learning station time to work with children who have been identified as needing her specialized services. Other personnel who work with the classroom teacher through collaboration and team teaching are the teachers of gifted education, Chapter 1, and English as a Second Language. When it is appropriate, students who need special services receive them in the classroom.

Earlier you mentioned parent reaction to this type of classroom when you described why contracts are used with students when they work in the learning stations. How does a teacher help parents understand what the educational objectives are in the classroom? The answer is twofold. First, teachers want parents to feel that they are partners, that they share the responsibility for their children's learning. A Parent Corner provides parents with checkout kits of simple learning activities, games, and books that children and parents can enjoy together. Parents are encouraged to support their child's learning at home. A monthly calendar is sent home with quick things parents and children can do daily, and an effort is made to provide a positive environment where parents feel welcome to visit and become involved. This involvement goes beyond helping with field trips and parties; parents are involved in policymaking and help as tutors, guest speakers, and providers of learning station materials, even as carpenters. Second, teacher and parents collaborate on the evaluation of their child's progress. Input is sought from parents regarding their opinion of their child's progress and evidence is shared of authentic assessment that has taken place in class—anecdotal notes that have been taken, the child's reading and writing logs, pictures or videotapes of student-completed projects, and dated work samples. Every child has a working and cumulative portfolio. The teacher communicates with all parents through newsletters and narrative student progress reports. In addition, positive notes and telephone calls are used to share student successes. When the curriculum is interesting, engaging, and developmentally appropriate, children are happy and excited about their learning. When parents understand the program and see their child's progress, they become the best public relation agents a teacher could ever hope for.

You have only spent the morning in this multiage class, but this short amount of time should convince you that multiaging is an appropriate model for the education of young children. This observation shows that successful multiage classrooms will require rethinking of many traditional teaching practices and special training, but the benefits to the students and their families will be well worth the effort.

Guiding and Managing:
The Administrator's Role

Who Is the Principal?

The role of the school-building-level administrator, the principal, has changed dramatically during the past 20 years. The traditional principal was a manager first and foremost. He or she (almost always he) directed everything that occurred at the school during the school calendar year, frequently with an iron hand. Instruction was a concern for many principals only when parents complained or if standardized test scores declined. Occasionally, a principal might read a story to a class, judge a contest, or visit a special activity, but the main focus of the job remained management.

This role, as we know, has been in transition for some time. The principal was forced to take on a much more active role in instruction, becoming the instructional leader of the school while still fulfilling the role of manager (Terry, 1987). It was at this point that the question "Who is the building administrator?" became a topic for research and study. Some of the best principals we know accepted both roles and worked very hard to be effective at each. They arrived at school very early to do paperwork and frequently stayed late after school to continue this work. During the school day, they changed hats and became instructional leaders, visiting classrooms, taking part in regular classroom activities, supervising a class while a teacher attended to some other need, and generally walking the halls. These principals knew what was going on in their buildings. Students knew their principal, and the principal knew the names of all students, not just the ones who visited the office on a regular basis for behavior problems. More females began moving into administrative roles, possibly because of the times, but also possibly because they were more comfortable with the role of instructional leader.

Today, as the overall organizational structure of the elementary school is in transition, the role of the principal is changing once again. The purpose of this chapter is to look at the role of the administrator in a school that includes multiage classrooms. The job still includes both managerial and instructional responsibilities, but the specifics are a bit different. If you wish to initiate the idea of adopting the multiage classroom in your building, there are many issues to consider.

Management

Organization

The principal working with multiage classrooms must deal with some of the same basic aspects of the original role, but with a different twist. This type of classroom has different needs. Some of these needs can be met within the regular school budget, but some cannot, especially as the transition to this style takes place. Multiage classrooms require more organization and planning, not less (Cohen, 1990).

Multiage classes must be organized to represent a truly heterogeneous grouping of students. In the past, combined classes frequently represented a collection of students from two grade levels, each group containing students from the "top" intellectual level, so that one group could work silently while the teacher directed instruction for the other students (Lodish, 1992). Multiage classes should not reflect any type of permanent, specialized grouping technique in their makeup other than random selection of students from two or more age levels. Flexible grouping for instruction and activities within the classroom is necessary to meet the individual needs of students (Stone, 1994/1995).

Scheduling

Scheduling for multiage classrooms should be a concern for the principal. One of the problems for many teachers during the school day is interruptions caused by extra class requirements such as physical education, library, and music. Although teachers enjoy the few minutes of break time that these class extras may give them during the day, it is hard to plan lessons around these breaks. This concern is even more important for the multiage classroom because activities in this atmosphere frequently require large uninterrupted spaces of time.

One way to deal with this problem for multiage classes is to schedule these class extras either early or late in the day, so as to leave large blocks of time. A further consideration should be an attempt to schedule classes for the same team of teachers at the same time so that those precious minutes can be used for team planning. Time for team planning is probably the number one concern of teachers in multiage settings. Without this consideration in scheduling, the only alternate times for team planning are before school, after school, or during lunch (if teachers do not have to monitor the lunchroom and/or the playground).

Another consideration is how to build or schedule teams of teachers. You might let teachers group themselves, but there are other issues to consider. Will teachers who select their own team do the best job together? Although teachers in a team should get along, areas of equal consideration should be whether they will work well together and provide each student with the best learning situation. Sometimes it may be more important to balance the strength of the teams to produce the best overall results.

Facilities

Facilities for the multiage classroom are an important consideration as this type of class works best when there is flexibility in the environment. Chairs and tables are preferable to desks, especially the all-in-one chair desk. Most schools do not have the money to toss school desks and buy a truckload of tables and chairs. One temporary remedy is to place three to five student desks together to form a student "table." Floors need carpet so students can use floor space. Until wall-to-wall carpet can be afforded, carpet samples or various sizes of area rugs can be used to make that cold tile more inviting. Some schools have made classrooms accessible to one another by opening up doorways in common walls. This allows for ease of student movement between room areas without constant hallway movement. Schools with flexible or movable walls between rooms find this to be a major plus when working with multiage classes. Families or teams of teachers who work together to teach and plan need to be placed in rooms that are next to or across the hall from one another so that movement from common lessons is cut to a minimum.

Materials

The multiage classroom has material needs that are quite different from those of the traditional graded system. A multiage classroom will include at least two age levels, requiring materials, therefore, for at least those two levels. However, because the whole philosophy behind the multiage classroom is to meet individual needs and development, that classroom may actually need materials for several levels. Each year, the materials needed will change as children in that room change, in terms of both developmental level and student turnover as some children move to another class.

This type of class uses lots of hands-on materials, both reusable and consumable. The simple basic student materials list of the past is greatly expanded to include items such as collections of children's literature, text sets, manipulatives, posters, a wide variety of art materials, computer and technology needs (video- and audiotapes, computer programs, and printer materials), and items for activity and learning centers. In the past, as these materials have crept into the classroom and gained in usage, teachers have reached deep into their own pockets to purchase these items. In preparing for an effective multiage program, administrators should map out and aggressively follow a plan to provide needed materials. Materials do not make the lesson, but without the basics, change is difficult.

Leadership

Role as Facilitator

To make the transition from a traditional graded elementary program to a multiage program, a school must have a guide or facilitator. This is usually the principal acting in the role of instructional leader for the school. Although other faculty members may be very excited about and willing to help direct the change, the principal must be a driving force for that change to take place. For the multiage classroom to be a success, the principal must guide teachers through the process (Stone, 1994/1995).

Planning the Process

Part of the facilitator's role is to help the affected faculty plan out a process, a sequence of events leading up to the implementation of the multiage classroom (Anderson, 1993). An example of this type of process might include the following steps: faculty reading and study, visitation to multiage class sites, faculty planning sessions, attendance at inservice sessions and conferences, and parent/community information sessions. All the desired steps in the process should be completed before the actual implementation. One school piloted a K-6, whole school, whole language program. The principal and faculty spent 3 years preparing for that first year, figuring out what they wanted to do and how to do it. At the end of the first year, not only had the school completed a very successful year of whole language instruction, but the standardized test scores for the school were greatly improved. Had they rushed into the process, it is possible they would have had far less success.

Being a Team Player

The facilitator must also consider him- or herself as a colleague, a member of the overall team that is working for success in this new program. Working as one more educator to develop a program to meet the needs of students, the "principal as director" role changes to one of "principal as helper." What do the teams of teachers need to help make the program work? How can the principal within his or her role of manager help to take down the barriers to change? Roll up your sleeves and get in the middle of the process, learning with the rest of the faculty. Remember, you are going to be one of the people with the responsibility of explaining the program to parents and community members, answering questions, defending the whole idea. You had better know what you are talking about!

Supporting the Process

As facilitator, you must also be the person who provides encouragement, feedback, and support, more support than in traditionally organized schools (Cohen, 1990). This is not going to be an easy process. There are going to be good days and not so good days. You must be ready with suggestions and take the time to visit with teachers and support their work. Once again, you have to know about and understand the process and the program. The administrator and the teachers must constantly remember that the multiage classroom brings with it a shift from teaching curriculum to teaching students (Black, 1993; Stone, 1994/1995).

Teacher Selection

Although the area of teacher selection may be considered to be part of the principal's managerial role, we suggest that it fits as part of the instructional leadership role, especially when approaching a new program such as the multiage classroom. This responsibility may also be shared by members of a site- and school-based decision-making council if your school is organized in this manner.

What should the principal be looking for in a teacher to teach in a multiage classroom? Such a teacher must be flexible, able to work with several age levels of students, able to change directions in planned instruction in order to address the teachable moment, and accepting of change. A teacher of a multiage class must be child centered in his or her approach to teaching. Black (1993) describes such teachers as "those who believe students learn by being active and engaged, thoughtful and reflective—rather than sitting passively or doing rote assignments" (p. 17). This person must be open to team planning and sharing of materials, and ready to visit with parents regularly. Because there is a lack of materials and curriculum specifically developed for multiage classrooms, prospective teachers must be prepared to strike out and develop needed items on their own (Cohen, 1990).

The principal of the whole language school mentioned earlier asked for and gained permission from the school board office to advertise for and interview all teachers who were interested in participating in the pilot project. Those in the school who wanted to stay, could. Those who did not want to be part of a whole language school were moved to other elementary schools. The faculty members who studied whole language and subsequently implemented their planned program all wanted to be there.

We do not suggest that all schools follow this example. However, it is important that the teachers who initially start the multiage program want to be involved with it. Then, slowly, the holdouts can be convinced through watching the success of the program.

Public Relations

Provide Information and Access

As already mentioned, it is very important to communicate with parents and other community members about a move to multiage grouping. When traditional programs are questioned or changed, uncertainty and resistance will occur, and it will be the job of the administrator to defend, explain, and answer questions about the new program.

One way to head off parents' concerns is to provide programs at school to explain and discuss the proposed changes. More than one program will be necessary, as not all parents and interested community members will be able to come at the same time. Some people will be unable to come at night. Videotape the presentation and the question and answer session. Make several copies and provide them for checkout so parents can view the program at home.

Another method to get out the message is to send parents a newsletter that includes basic information about the program and advertises the availability of the videos. Remember, however, that some parents do not read, some are not comfortable reading, and others do not have time to read a long document. Make the information basic and to the point.

Ask parents to call you if they have questions. Invite parents to visit the school and the classrooms once they are in place. Each month, invite 10 or 12 parents or community members, for lunch and a classroom visit. Make people feel that there is nothing to hide, and they will be less likely to look for problems.

Multiage, active, involved classrooms are going to produce wonderful student products as a result of daily opportunities to read and write (Stone, 1994/1995). Look for ways to show these products off to the community, whether they are art projects, student-written books, class-produced plays, or new ways to learn math facts. Celebrate the students' successes with everyone!

Student Placement

Parents are going to be concerned about having their children placed in a classroom for 2 or more years with the same teacher. It is your job to help parents see the positives in this type of placement. They will need to see that teachers will get to know children and their learning styles so that at the beginning of succeeding years teachers will need less time to get to know students and to acclimate students to the classroom. Students already will be secure in their environments and ready to learn (Black, 1993).

Occasionally, a teacher and a student may not work well together. Their respective teaching and learning styles may not mesh well. Or there may be a conflict between teacher and student or parent and teacher. The principal must be ready to work out such a situation for the good of the student. A different placement may be needed. Listening to all parties with an objective ear is the key to resolving such situations.

The Decision to Change and Beyond

Depending on the organizational structure of your school, the decision to make the change to multiage classrooms may be made by a variety of people from the principal, to the faculty as a whole, to the curriculum committee, to a school-based decision-making council, or a combination of these. The principal becomes the supporter, the defender, and the cheerleader of the change.

What Do We Do Now?

Once the decision has been made, training must begin. Find a knowledgeable consultant to help your faculty learn about multiage classrooms. Decide on and obtain some professional books for a professional school library to which faculty can refer. Locate individuals to do specific inservice programs in areas such as continuous progress, authentic assessment, whole language, thematic instruction, and curriculum integration. See if you can locate training programs that some of your faculty members can attend to become more aware of the new program. Seek out a school nearby that has a successful multiage program and send faculty members to visit. As a faculty, you may wish to have everyone read the same materials and hold after-school seminars where open discussion can take place.

Remember, you are all taking a risk. Every voice needs to be heard and considered. And even when the process is in place and multiage classrooms are happening in your school, the process of change usually will not lead to immediate success. Change takes time (Anderson, 1993; Black, 1993)! Continue to meet to work out problems that arise and to support one another.

Misinformation, Misconceptions, and Obstacles

As you begin to work with the multiage classroom concept, you will find that some people will have misconceptions about multiage grouping. Lodish (1992) describes the following four common misconceptions:

1. Multiage vertical groups are less structured than single-grade horizontal ones.
2. Mixed-age classrooms are meant to equalize children of different ages and abilities.
3. The younger child in a mixed-age class will be "stretched" more than in a single-age class.
4. Once children begin a mixed-age class in the lower of two grades, they must stay with the class for the second year.

In response, let us look at each item. First, the multiage organization actually requires more, not less, organization because the teacher must plan and organize for the individual needs of each child, teaching the child first. Second, this type of classroom offers students who represent a wide range of rates of progress and abilities the opportunity to interact and work together. Third, all students can be challenged when the curriculum is equally demanding at all levels and addresses individual academic levels and learning styles. Fourth, as mentioned earlier, if student-teacher problems arise, a change in placement may be a consideration. Some schools, recognizing that not all students learn best in the same environment, have kept some traditional classrooms. In some cases, placement in a traditional, horizontally structured classroom may be an option for the next year for a student (Lodish, 1992).

Tradition may be an obstacle to acceptance of the multiage classroom. Parents may not understand at what level their child is working when there are no "grade" levels. It is very important that there be no grade connotations whatsoever if this classroom organization is to work (Pavan, 1992). Many parents expect their children to compete for good grades, working to do better than other students. They may be very suspicious of the cooperative nature of the multiage classroom. But one of the major premises of this classroom is cooperation, not competition, so that all can learn (Cohen, 1990; Dever, Zila, & Manzano, 1994; Stone, 1994/1995). Students have always used textbooks and followed a single-grade curriculum (Black, 1993). Materials will be very different in a multiage classroom. Although some textbooks may still be in use, they usually will be for reference use and will be only one of many materials available to the teacher and students.

The biggest obstacle to the implementation of the multiage classroom may be the teacher or teachers who are not sold on the idea. Frequently, these are teachers who have taught for 10 to 15 years and who are comfortable with what they have been doing. The idea of change, of starting over and learning a new way, can be frightening, if not overwhelming. You, as initiator of this idea, must find ways to help teachers learn about, get excited about, and want to take on the change involved in the transition. It is hoped that most of the teachers in your building will get excited about the multiage classroom. If some cannot, then follow the solution of the whole language principal and attempt to build a faculty that will support the change. Once you have a faculty that is behind the idea, you will be able to show a united team to parents and the community.

What Change Will Bring

Once the decision to make the change has been made, you may wonder what reasonable expectations you can have for the first year. Remember that students in a multiage classroom develop and progress at their own individual rates and that, therefore, the classroom will be a good example of continuous progress working right there in your building. For students to develop and learn at their own rates, DAP must be in use in the classroom (Black, 1993; Stone, 1994/1995).

It may seem that teachers have to actively develop a separate set of plans for each student, like an individual education plan (IEP) for every child in the classroom. Once teachers become familiar with their students, however, they will begin to form short-term small groupings to address areas of need. These groups will constantly change as individual students move on to the next skill, idea, concept, or assignment. At first it will not be obvious, but students will soon realize that they are learning in an environment free of failure and anxiety (Black, 1993). In this type of setting, students can relax and concentrate on learning at their own pace.

Teachers will find that the multiage classroom will work, but only with a great deal of effort on their part. They will need to put a lot more time into planning and preparation and, as a result, must be committed to the ideas behind the multiage classroom.

Pulling It All Together

Pavan (1992) tells us that the benefits to be gained through a nongraded (multiage) format increase as students spend more and more time in this type of classroom. Boys, African American students, underachievers, and students of lower socioeconomic status appear to benefit the most from this organization (Goodlad &

Anderson, 1987). Miller (1991a) states that areas such as student attitudes and peer relations are greatly improved with multiage grouping. All these things are possible, given time, hard work, good organization, and lots of support from the administrator.

It is up to you and your faculty to decide what direction to take. Keep in mind what other new programs or requirements are being expected of your faculty. Take the time to make a good decision. Once the decision has been made to proceed with the multiage classroom, keep in mind the ideas we have suggested, and develop a step-by-step process you and your faculty can follow toward success. Make sure *you* are right in the middle of the process. And buy some happy face stickers for those days that seem like they will never end. Happy planning!

The Multiage Classroom:
Questions and Comments

Following our discussion of how a multiage classroom organization will make your school different and successful, we thought the reader might like to hear responses to this idea from the field. After brainstorming ideas for questions to present to individuals, we selected the following four questions to elicit as objective a picture as possible:

1. Does the multiage classroom help children in the learning process? Why or why not?
2. If you had to name one characteristic of the multiage classroom setting that is best, what would it be?
3. If you could make one suggestion to a principal and/or school considering the multiage classroom organization, what would that be?
4. What has been the hardest thing to overcome as you have made this change? The easiest?

To gain a cross section of responses, we interviewed a variety of people from a number of locations. These individuals included relatively new teachers, experienced teachers, principals, parents, and other members of the public.

Question 1

When writing Question 1, our intent was to zero in on the needs of students and to try to gain input as to whether this "new" classroom organization addresses those needs in a better or more complete fashion. It is hoped that all the groups of individuals questioned would want to help children learn to their best capability. To the question, "Does the multiage classroom help children in the learning process? Why or why not?" the following responses were given.

Teacher Responses

Yes! It allows for exploration of the different aspects of learning. Each child has the opportunity to progress at his or her own level in his or her own way.

For some children (the outgoing, self-confident ones), multiage classrooms can be a plus, and the information they acquire can be put to use. However, most children feel the older ones are smarter, and their self-concepts suffer because they "don't know" as much as their peers.

Yes and no. Most children thrive in the multiage classroom with well-prepared teachers. The students who lack skills learn so much from older students. Older students practice what they've learned by tutoring younger students. Everyone works at their own rate. Students who need a structured learning environment don't do well.

Yes, all children have an equal chance at learning.

Yes, because children are allowed or should be allowed to progress at their own rate; also, children of different ages and abilities learn to interact with each other [promoting diversity].

I feel that the multiage classroom is very beneficial to the learning process because the children learn to work together, they work at their own level, and they become more independent and responsible.

The multiage classroom makes the students more responsible, independent, and more willing to cooperate with others. It also makes them better thinkers, speakers, and listeners because they are responsible for sharing their ideas as well as listening to the ideas of others.

I think the multiage classroom helps children to learn because they are allowed to work on their own level rather than being expected to "keep up" with everyone else.

As a special education teacher of elementary children with learning disabilities, mild mental deficiencies, and emotional-behavior problems, I have worked with multiage groups for 6 school years. In my position, I feel that this grouping does help in the learning process. The older children help teach the younger children, they motivate them, and they can explain things in a different way. The younger children provide a means of enabling the older ones to feel better about themselves and to practice previously learned skills.

Yes. Students are allowed to interact with peers of different abilities. Strengths and weaknesses of all are a shared experience. Students need this experience because it closely resembles real-life activities.

The different ages of the children are an asset in bringing out different ideas and thoughts to the lessons. The children learn a great deal from each other.

Administrative Responses

Yes, even if we have students near the same chronological age, they are not necessarily equal in mental ability. In the long run, the multiage classroom gives us the ability to provide more age-appropriate instruction to larger populations.

When used appropriately, multiage classrooms can be very beneficial to students. [Students] are not pressured to do more than they can and should be able to feel a part of the classroom no matter what their ability level.

Most definitely! In the ungraded primary, students have the opportunity to learn a greater variety of things than when they were ability grouped.

Public Responses

Yes, it lets the children learn from others with different ages and experiences.

Yes, it can be a big help with the older, more mature children who can help other children who may be having trouble.

No, because the goals for the children are not clearly laid out. Expectations are not always clear.

Yes, because if the children need it they can review topics as necessary.

Yes, the other children get a chance to interact with other age groups and get different perspectives.

I believe it helps some children. No curriculum meets the needs of all children. With some middle ground, I think this may be a significant step in the right direction.

Parent Responses

Yes, the multiage classroom gives children the opportunity to work with other children both older and younger than they are. I feel that the children can learn from each other as well as the teacher.

I prefer the single-graded classroom. It's too hard for a teacher to try to teach to so many different ages.

The multiage setting is not working in some classrooms. The students aren't being allowed to work at their own level. My daughter spends most of her day helping other students with their work. Her spelling tests are far too simple and I don't feel like she is being challenged enough.

Sometimes, I do feel that your above-average children need to be challenged more.

The multiage classroom may help children learn because [ideally] it fosters cooperative learning.

Yes, I feel [my child] gains more insight and knowledge from his peers. He looks up to them because they are older.

The multiage classroom helps children who are already bright and eager to learn. It discourages slower children.

The multiage classroom does not help children. It limits gifted children in an attempt to help slower learners.

I cannot say for sure, because I work a lot at home to compensate for anything I feel my child may be missing.

Learning in the multiage classroom has a lot to do with the teacher. If the teacher is interested in teaching in the ungraded primary, then I think learning occurs; if [teachers] are not interested, then learning does not occur.

Question 2

Many times, as we look at change and new programs, all we can see are the problems and issues of concern. Question 2 asks for positive input. It asks, "If you had to name one characteristic of the multiage classroom setting that is best, what would it be?" This question requires the respondent to think positively, to look for "good" in change. The same four groups responded to this question in the following manner.

Teacher Responses

Collaboration.

The ability to do more cooperative learning experiences. This teaches students to get along with one another.

Peer tutoring.

The older children do help the younger and can be a great help in the learning environment.

It allows the higher intelligence children to move on to challenging material. However, they are often used as peer tutors and do not get to move ahead at a pace they could.

Flexibility of teaching, keeping some students more than 1 year.

Centers—children have the best of everything: cooperate with one another, do independent learning.

The team teaching is definitely a plus, it is fun to work with other teachers to share ideas and lessons.

The "teachable moments." Being able to watch children work and learn together.

All kids seem to have improved self-esteem.

The best aspect of the multiage classroom, in my opinion, is the way that everything is student centered.

The self-motivation I see in my students. I enjoy seeing them work to improve themselves with little or no need for encouragement from me.

Cooperative learning.

I like the way the teaching/learning strategies have become more individualized.

I like the idea that students have lots of hands-on opportunities and the freedom to move around. Children of primary age have an innate need to do so.

Administrative Responses

Variety of instruction that *must* be implemented in order to meet the needs of all students.

I as an administrator like the fact that we don't have to deal with negative retention. We can now explain to parents that their child has not met necessary milestones and that another year working with same-ability-level students can catch them up, yet the child does not have as much of a blow to his or her self-esteem.

Peer tutoring.

The independence that it teaches the children. It teaches responsibility.

Students work at individual levels.

Public Responses

Active learning.

Peers can help each other.

Diversity.

Different resources that would be available for a variety of age groups.

Peer tutoring and more hands-on activities.

I would have to say the hands-on experiences that allow for better understanding than just textbooks allowed.

My granddaughter tells me she likes working in her "family."

Parent Responses

The wide range of abilities and how the students work together to "get the job done."

The students seem to be able to work well together.

I am pleased with the emphasis on reading. During recreational reading time, the students read to others as well as listen to others read to them. I think this is very important.

I think it makes the older children feel good helping the younger children.

Cooperative learning.

Peer collaborating.

Stimulation of mixed age groups.

Multiage class works well for slow learners.

That the younger children benefit more from the tutoring done by the older children.

Question 3

Suggestions from the field are a very important component of the process of perfecting a change in the schools. If you return to the four-step process of curriculum development, this same process seems appropriate here as you develop multiage classrooms. We analyze what our needs are, we design according to those needs, we implement what is designed, and we evaluate the new ideas, looking for positive and negative aspects so that continuous improvement can be made. Question 3—"If you could make one suggestion to a principal and/or school considering the multiage classroom organization, what would that be?"—elicits input that can be used to help plan the entire process. Responses include the following.

Teacher Responses

Better allotment of funds.

Teachers need to be more willing to share responsibilities and materials.

Keep kindergarten separate to provide for social skills needs. Integrate for short periods of time in multiage classrooms.

Have plenty of aides and help in the classroom. One teacher *cannot* meet everyone's needs and do what is expected.

More team teacher planning time. Using teacher teams more effectively.

Please give parents a choice in every school between multiage and traditional classrooms.

My suggestion would be for all parties to go into it with positive attitudes. Everyone involved must be flexible and willing to change if necessary.

I would suggest that everyone involved be very open-minded, be willing to take risks, make mistakes, and learn from their mistakes.

Anyone thinking about this type of classroom organization should be willing to make many changes and learn from your mistakes.

I would suggest that they hire as much help as possible as well as push for volunteers. The more help you can get in a classroom, the more individual attention the students will get.

Group children so that there are enough strong, above-average-ability children to compensate for the weaker, below-average children.

I would suggest that schools do a lot of planning before getting started. They need to consider curriculum, space, budgets, class sizes, materials, and the students to be served.

Administrative Responses

Lay aside preconceived attitudes and expect success.

I would suggest to a school considering the change that they make sure the teachers are comfortable with what is happening. It is unfair to a teacher to not be supportive of their concerns and fears.

Smaller class size, kindergarten separate, but mixed in and out during the week for short periods of time.

I know that in some schools that they really aren't multiaged, so to speak. If it is going to be a true ungraded primary, we must *all* do multiage grouping.

Public Responses

Plan thoroughly before beginning the process.

Maybe a little more discipline.

Organize the classroom so that the new students are not intimidated.

Don't forget the older children in multiage classrooms. They aren't being peer tutored. Often they are "extra" teachers, which is fine if they are also continuing to be challenged academically.

I would suggest that they keep the community better informed about what this type of classroom is, what is happening in these types of classrooms, etc.

Parent Responses

I think it is very important to educate the parents about this new organization. Parents will be more likely to accept the change if they know what is going on in the classroom.

I would suggest that they train their teachers well to teach this way and keep the parents informed about what is going on.

Teachers need to be well educated on this type of teaching before they attempt to teach in the multiage setting.

I think you should have one grade level or if you have two grade levels in one room the teacher should have help [aide].

Prepare teachers well and give them a lot of help. Be sure your teachers really want to make the change.

There should not be more than 1 year's difference in age of groups.

Prepare teacher for the change.

Request that the teachers have more aides or parent volunteers to help in the classroom.

More materials. Sarah is always taking things from the house that she needs at school.

Question 4

Realistically, there are going to be ups and downs to any change in the educational process. Question 4—"What has been the hardest thing to overcome as you have made this change? The easiest?"—allows respondents to focus on the highs and lows of adopting the multiage classroom. The following responses provide a varied picture.

Teacher Responses

The hardest thing is that when working in groups, because of the variety of attention spans, I have difficulty keeping their attention. Easiest would be their eagerness to do activities.

Easiest: already doing thematic teaching, fly-by-the-seat-of-your-pants teaching with no textbooks or workbooks. Hardest: helping kindergartners adjust to school and multiage classes.

Meeting the needs of every child with such a "wide range." Easiest: the older children with a greater ability helping with the younger ones.

Hardest: meeting needs of all students at all levels, one-room-schoolhouse effect. Easiest: older students help younger students.

Planning unit work to include Ks is the easiest. Locating materials for themes and units is the hardest.

Hardest is allowing the children to learn on their own and teaching cooperative learning skills. The easiest is throwing away the textbooks.

Hardest: adapting years of materials to fit the primary program.

Easiest: student acclimation and watching children learn through their own learning style. Hardest: attitudes of teachers, administrators, and parents.

The hardest thing to overcome was the assessment. At first, I wasn't sure how to assess children who were all working at their own level. However, once I learned to compare a student only to himself or herself, the process became quite a bit easier.

The frequent "working noise" was a little hard to get used to at first, but it later proved to be very productive. The easiest thing was working with the students at their own level.

The hardest thing for me with multiage grouping is selecting activities and materials that are appropriate for all. The easiest is getting the children to help each other and work together.

The hardest thing to overcome at first was allowing the students to make many choices. However, once I saw how their choices were becoming more responsible, I was convinced that this is very important. The easiest thing to overcome was letting the students work together and learn from each other.

The hardest thing to overcome to the change of primary school is that it seems to be changing constantly. That could be a good thing for the students, but as a teacher, I find it hard to adjust. The easiest thing about the switch to primary school is that things seem more flexible with the entire school community. I think this is best for the kids.

Administrative Responses

Hardest: teacher and parental attitudes. Easiest: acclimation of students.

Having been a first-grade teacher for many years, it was hard for me not to be in the action of the classroom during the change. As an administrator, it was hard to help teachers with the sudden transition. The best part for me has been seeing it all come together and be successful.

The hardest—change is difficult, especially such comprehensive change in a short amount of time.

The hardest change we have had to make in the multiage classroom is getting the parents to understand the transition to the ungraded primary. We have also had trouble getting materials ready for the classes each year due to differences in each group. The easiest change has been how well the children have adapted to the new environment.

The hardest obstacle is teacher attitude. The easiest part of the change is students' attitudes.

Public Responses

Hardest: public misunderstanding. Easiest: producing appropriate learning materials.

All ages of children are in one class. Cooperative learning.

Hardest: negative publicity. Easiest: classroom arrangement.

The change [in the teacher's role] from being the authority figure to the facilitator. Also, the amount of time needed to plan has changed dramatically!

I think the hardest thing is moving from the textbooks to the "box it—bag it" type of instruction. The easiest would be that at this tender age, most children are able to adapt to changes.

I know my granddaughter likes it; she likes to go to school.

Parent Responses

The hardest part of the change was that I was afraid my child was being used as a "guinea pig" for trying out this new way of learning. But once I saw how the program works, I think it's great!

I am most concerned about how my child will make the transition into intermediate, which is much more structured than the primary block.

I do not like the new grading system. I would feel more comfortable seeing letter grades simply because that is what I am used to.

Hardest: I think planning for children on all different levels would be difficult. Easiest: students adjusting to the change.

The hardest would be changing the attitudes and expectations of adults—parents and teachers. The easiest would be changing the patterns for the children.

It hasn't been necessary to overcome anything!

Hardest obstacle is the lack of grades. Parents feel like they are not getting enough information about their children's progress.

The hardest obstacle was reassuring students.

The hardest is knowing there is no structure in the classroom. The easiest is when my child is a part of the younger age of the class, and he will be exposed to a higher level of academics.

The easiest thing for us is that Sarah enjoys going to school. I enjoy helping her with activities she has to do when she brings them home. The hardest thing for us has been that Sarah has no textbooks; when she has a problem with something, she does not have a textbook to refer to in order to help her with her problems. I would like to see them have more textbooks.

A Final Word

Making a move to multiage classrooms is a big step for any school. As with any change, people will be unsure, suspicious, and questioning of this new idea. Some are going to be far more willing to take the "giant step" to change, and to accept change, than others. The intent of this book is to provide enough information about the multiage classroom, where the idea came from, why we are using it today—what it looks like, and how it affects all of the individuals involved—so that you can decide if you want to consider this organizational structure for your school. An annotated bibliography of additional reading selections follows, should you desire more information. We hope that you will decide to use the multiage classroom in your setting. It can provide a wonderful opportunity for students and teachers to learn and enjoy the process. Remember now, be flexible, listen, enjoy, read, and have fun. . . . Good luck!

Annotated Bibliography
and References

Annotated Bibliography

Anderson, R. H. (1993). The return of the nongraded classroom. *Principal, 72*(3), 9-12.

The author explains why our schools became graded and why we are now returning to heterogeneous multiage grouping.

Anderson, R. H. (1987). Shaping up the shop: How school organization influences teaching and learning. *Educational Leadership, 44*(5), 45.

Anderson stresses the importance of considering the multiage classroom when discussing school improvement.

Bredekamp, S., & Shepard, L. (1989). How best to protect children from inappropriate school expectations, practices, and policies. *Young Children, 44*(3), 14-24.

The article discusses strategies that have been used to protect children from inappropriate practices that have not worked and proposes alternatives.

Charlesworth, R. (1989). "Behind" before they start? *Young Children, 44*(3), 5-13.

Charlesworth describes four methods designed to help prevent kindergarten failure, one of which involves multiage groupings.

Chase, P., & Doan, J. (1994). *Full circle: A new look at multi-age education.* Portsmouth, NH: Heinemann.

This publication allows the reader to see the inside of multiage classrooms from both a research and practice point of view.

Connell, D. R. (1987). The first 30 years were the fairest: Notes from the kindergarten and ungraded primary (K-1-2). *Young Children, 42*(5), 30-39.

The article discusses curriculum content for the early grades.

Cushman, K. (1990). The whys and hows of the multi-age classroom. *American Educator, 14*(2), 28-32, 39.

Cushman discusses the advantages of the multiage classroom and suggests methods of grouping.

Davies, A., & Politano, C. (1994). *Building connections: Multi-age and more.* Winnipeg, Manitoba: Peguis.

This book reflects the experiences of two teachers who have taught in a multiage setting for a number of years.

Evangelou, D. (1989). Mixed-age groups in early childhood education. *ERIC Digest* (ED 308 990)

The topic of mixed-age groups is discussed in terms of advantages, social development, cognitive development, and implications for young children.

Glover, M. K. (1993). *Two years: A teacher's memoir.* Portsmouth, NH: Heinemann.

Glover takes the reader into her classroom of first and second graders and talks about what works and doesn't work.

Griffin, A. (1994). Multiple conversations in a multi-age classroom. *Talking Points, 5*(3), 6-7.

Griffin relates some student conversations from her K-1 classroom and talks about the multiage classroom.

Gutierrez, R., & Slavin, R. (1992). Achievement effects of the nongraded elementary school: A best evidence synthesis. *Review of Educational Research, 62*(4), 333-376.

Gutierrez and Slavin summarize achievement results from multiage classrooms.

Hunter, M. C. (1992). *How to change to a nongraded school.* Alexandria, VA: Association for Supervision and Curriculum Development.

This text provides a roadmap to help a school change from the traditional format to a multiage classroom organizational structure.

Kantrowitz, B., & Wingert, P. (1989, April 17). How kids learn. *Newsweek,* pp. 50-56.

This article talks about changing the ways schools teach children, from drill in desks to moving, exploring, and touching.

Kasten, W. (1994). Compelling reasons for multi-age classrooms. *Talking Points, 5*(3), 2-5.

Kasten reports her research findings from interviews and visitations and explores many of the variables to consider when using this form of organization.

Kasten, W. C., & Clarke, B. K. (1993). *The multi-age classroom: A family of learners.* Katonah, NY: Richard C. Owens.

The authors discuss all aspects of the multiage classroom, including understanding the model, benefits, the classroom as a community, and actually implementing the program.

Kelley, M. F., & Surbeck, E. (1991). *Restructuring early childhood education. Fastback 329.* Bloomington, IN: Phi Delta Kappa Educational Foundation.

This booklet examines how to go about reaching the national goal of having all children ready to learn when they start school.

Kindley, M. (1985). Little schools on the prairie still teach a big lesson. *Smithsonian, 16*(7), 118-131.

This text discusses current teaching experiences in a one-room school and relates input from parents.

Miller, B. A. (1990). A review of the quantitative research on multigrade instruction. *Research in Rural Education, 7*(1), 1-8.

Miller reports the findings from 21 quantitative studies regarding student achievement in multigrade versus single-grade classrooms and discusses other noncognitive areas.

Surbeck, E. (1992). Multi-age programs in primary grades: Are they educationally appropriate? *Childhood Education, 69*(1), 3-4.

Surbeck explains the importance of understanding the rationale behind multiage grouping and addresses some factors that influence successful programs.

References

Anderson, R. (1993). The return of the nongraded classroom. *Principal, 72*(3), 9-12.

Aulgur, L., Baker, L., & Copeland, K. (1992). Multi-age classrooms: Option to an outdated system. *Teachers Networking: The Whole Language Newsletter, 11*(2), 2-4.

Black, S. (1993). Beyond age and grade. *The Executive Educator, 15*(9), 17-20.

Blount, H. (1992). The one-room school: Remembering and reinventing. *Reading Improvement, 29*(3), 179-182.

Brewer, J. A. (1995). *Introduction to early childhood education: Preschool through primary grades.* Needham Heights, MA: Allyn & Bacon.

Bridge, C. A. (1994). *Primary thoughts: Implementing Kentucky's primary program.* Frankfort: Kentucky Department of Education.

Burruss, B. (1993). *The primary school: A resource guide for parents.* Lexington, KY: The Prichard Committee for Academic Excellence and the Partnership for Kentucky School Reform.

Cohen, D. (1990). A look at multi-age classrooms. *Education Digest, 55*(9), 20-23.

Cohen, J. (1986). Theoretical consideration of peer tutoring. *Psychology in the Schools, 23*, 175-186.

Daniel, T. C. (1994). Prerequisites for collaborative thematic instruction between primary and physical education teachers. *Kentucky Association for Health, Physical Education, Recreation and Dance Journal, 30*(2), 25-27.

Dever, M., Zila, R., & Manzano, N. (1994). Multiage classrooms: A new way to learn math. *Principal, 73*(4), 22, 24, 26.

Gardner, H. (1985). *Frames of mind: The theory of multiple intelligences.* New York: Basic Books.

Gatzke, M. (1991). Creating meaningful kindergarten programs. In B. Spodek (Ed.), *Educationally appropriate kindergarten practices* (pp. 97-109). Washington, DC: National Education Association.

Goodlad, J., & Anderson, R. (1987). *The non-graded elementary school* (Rev. ed.). New York: Teachers College Press.

Katz, L. G., & Chard, S. C. (1989). *Engaging children's minds: The project approach.* Norwood, NJ: Ablex.

Lodish, R. (1992). The pros and cons of mixed-age grouping. *Principal, 71*(5), 20-22.

Miller, B. (1991a). A review of the qualitative research on multiage instruction. *Journal of Research in Rural Education, 7*(2), 3-12.

Miller, B. (1991b). Teaching and learning in the multigrade classroom: Student performance and instructional routines. *ERIC Digest* (ED 335 178)

Muse, I., & Moore, R. (1988). One-room schools in America: Going, going, staying. *Small-Town, 18*(4), 9-13.

National Association for the Education of Young Children. (1987). *Developmentally appropriate practice in early childhood programs serving children from birth through age 8.* Washington, DC: Author.

Ornstein, A., & Hunkins, F. (1993). *Curriculum: Foundations, principles, and theory* (2nd ed.). Boston: Allyn & Bacon.

Pavan, B. (1992). The benefits of nongraded schools. *Educational Leadership, 50*(2), 22-25.

Planbook for meeting individual needs. (1995). Frankfort: Kentucky Department of Education.

Primary your way. (1995). Frankfort: Kentucky Department of Education.

Shepard, L. A., & Smith, M. L. (1986, November). Synthesis of research on school readiness and kindergarten retention. *Educational Leadership, 44*, 78-86.

Southern Regional Education Board. (1994). *Getting schools ready for children: The other side of the readiness goal.* Atlanta, GA: Author.

Stone, S. (1994/1995). Strategies for teaching children in multiage classrooms. *Childhood Education, 71*(2), 102-104.

Terry, K. (1987). Manager or leader: The quandary of the school principal. *Record in Educational Administration and Supervision, 7*(2), 15-17.

Transformations: Kentucky's curriculum framework. (1993). Frankfort: Kentucky Department of Education.

Wong, H. K. (1991). *The first days of school.* Sunnyvale, CA: Author.

**CORWIN
PRESS**

The Corwin Press logo—a raven striding across an open book—represents the happy union of courage and learning. We are a professional-level publisher of books and journals for K–12 educators, and we are committed to creating and providing resources that embody these qualities. Corwin's motto is "Success for All Learners."